MORE THAN JUST WORDS

The Bible Is God's Voice

REVEREND GORDON K. DAVIS

xulon PRESS

DEDICATION

This book is dedicated to the memory of my Grandmother who saw in me the possibility of one day being used by God for ministry. It is also dedicated to my wife Sharon who encouraged me to finish the book and to our children, Dyer, Curtis and Joy. Last but not least to my niece Vickie who edited *More Than Just Words*.

MORE THAN JUST WORDS
THE BIBLE IS GOD'S VOICE

"Oh for the breath of spiritual life"

WHAT IS THE END FOR WHICH
GOD CREATED THE WORLD?
—Jonathan Edwards

**WHAT IS THE END FOR WHICH
GOD CREATED YOU?**

CONTENTS

INTRODUCTION

Robert Frost once said, "You can be a little ungrammatical if you come from the right part of the country." I am beginning with this statement because it leads to a positive conclusion in my story. I hope it will make us think positively. Some people may want to read my last page first. It is with deep prayer and humility that I present this study about the Bible and its profound message concerning the Father and the Son and the Holy Spirit.

What I hope to accomplish in this book is to show how important it is to take time out from our busy lives to let God's VOICE calm our overstressed spirits by speaking to us personally from his Word. I hope to answer such questions as what is so important about God's interest in my life? The only way to get the answers we need concerning our questions—Who am I? Why am I here?— is to study the Bible. If you ask your neighbor or friends or anyone on the street they can't give you a good answer because we all are in the same boat. The answer has to come from outside our selves. We have to turn to God to get the authentic answers. Exactly what does God intend for my life? Fortunately God has left us with the revelation of himself in the Bible. Because of this revelation we can begin to understand who God is, where he came from, why he is here, and how his greatest desire is that your life be lived under his care. We are to worship him in spirit and in truth.

I spent well over two years of study and research putting this material together. I have prayed over it that God might find it useful and inspiring in the right hands . My primary goal is to leave some of my thoughts and insights for my friends, my children and grandchildren after I am with the Lord. I take full responsibility for what I have written. If any improvements or corrections are needed please make them on the margins but stay true to God's word. As Paul would say: "Grace and peace to you from the Lord Jesus Christ." In III John vs.2: "Beloved I pray that in all respects you may prosper and be in good health, just as your soul prospers."

Amen.

PART I

I HEAR GOD'S VOICE

Chapter 1

MY OWN PERSONAL EPIPHANY WITH GOD
MAY 28, 2013

I had a very interesting and provocative dream recently. I have been studying and praying often about somehow making God's word available to more people by impressing upon them how powerful his VOICE is and how God is reaching out to us. I try to spend one hour every day praying for friends and loved ones and asking God to use me according to his will.

One evening a few weeks ago, I went to bed and fell fast asleep. I began dreaming in the early morning hours before sunrise and suddenly my mind got stuck on praying for the lost souls in and out of my family. I was given a vision where God was speaking to me and I was concerned that no one was listening to him. I found myself praying for whoever came into my mind. I asked God why people were not listening to him? I became desperate and fearful. I told myself, *Why won't people take God's Word seriously?* They just won't listen. I was praying for my own family. At that moment in my dream I had an epiphany — They aren't listening because they don't realize the Bible is God's VOICE speaking directly to them. It is not just printed words on a page in a book with leather binding. It is God's VOICE speaking through the Holy Spirit. In my dream I fell on the floor weeping. The Bible is alive. At that moment I decided to write about the Bible and concentrate on God's VOICE through the Old and New Testament.

I have been guided to write about the critical value of taking God's VOICE seriously. My personal commentary is about God's VOICE bringing strong words of warning and comfort. He sends forth his Holy Spirit to be our guide to all his truth.

WHEN WILL WE BELIEVE AND ACCEPT THE FACT THAT THE BIBLE FROM GENESIS TO REVELATION IS GOD'S VOICE?

IT IS GOD'S VOICE FOR US.

Creation displays the glory of God. (Psalm 19) A newborn baby displays the glory of God. (Psalm 139) But the Bible is the only complete revelation we have that explains WHO God is and HOW we are to worship and enjoy him forever.

To begin I wish to share a selection of verses that are as alive today as when written:

Proverbs 5:12-13: *"How have I hated instruction, and my heart spurned reproof... I have not listened to the VOICE of my teachers, nor inclined my ear to my instructors."*

This is the lament of the person who has had the opportunity to hear the Word and listened to the VOICE of his teachers and decided to reject the truth. It is like the passenger who willingly missed the boat after the last call for boarding. It left the harbor without him. When we refuse to listen to God's Word there will be consequences. Listen to the VOICE of teachers. We were never meant to live independent of each other as God has put us together in a family and in a church body so that we can grow.

Isaiah 28:23: *"Give ear and hear my VOICE, listen and hear my words."*

Observe the progression from listen, give ear, hear my voice, mind gate, hearing gate to speech gate. God does not indulge man's interest for nothing. He means what he says and we better take heed.

Matthew 2:17-18: *"Then what has been spoken through Jeremiah the prophet was fulfilled," A VOICE was heard in Ramah, weeping and great mourning, Rachel weeping for her children, and she refuses to be comforted, because they are no more."*

This is in reference to Babylonian captivity (586 B.C.) forward to Herod's murdering of all the newborn infants of Israel. With tragedy there is mourning. No one suffers but what it affects us all. Stop and think of different disasters in your lifetime—Oklahoma, 9/11, the 1989 San Francisco earthquake, New Orleans' Katrina, on and on. During these times of disaster people are once again reminded that God is there and they seek comfort by returning to churches in droves. A few weeks or months they return to their old ways, leaving the church behind.

Mathew 3:3: *"For this is the one referred to by Isaiah the prophet when he said, the VOICE of one crying in*

13

the wilderness, make ready the way of the Lord, make His paths straight."

Both the Old Testament verb and the New Testament noun refer to the act of contrition and a turning away from sin. It is radical to consciously turn from sin and take the Gospel seriously. John the Baptist knew the Jews understood the meaning of heaven. They never used the name 'God' but spoke of heaven as a euphemism for God. John and Jesus made it clear that the kingdom is here and present in all who will believe in and receive Jesus Christ as Lord. The Holy Spirit now dwells in every true believer as a confirmation, a guarantee of the righteousness we receive by faith.

Matt. 3:16-17: *"After being baptized, Jesus came up immediately out of the water; and behold, the heavens were opened, and He saw the Spirit of God descending as a dove and lighting on Him, and behold, a VOICE out of the heavens said, "this is My beloved Son, in whom I AM well pleased."* Meditate on these words. Ask God to make them real to you.

John 5:25: *"Truly, truly, I say unto you, an hour is coming and now is, when the dead will hear the VOICE of the Son of God, and those who hear will live."*

Here is Christ's own testimony of his divine relationship with the Father:
- He is equal with God in his person (Vs.17-18)
- He is equal with God in his works (Vs.19-20)
- He is equal with God in his power and sovereignty (Vs.21)
- He is equal with God in his judgment (Vs.22)
- He is equal with God in his honor (Vs.23)

Jesus is equal with God in caring for you. All power and glory is in his hands. To the Father he says: "I in them and your in Me, that they may be perfected in unity, so that the world may know that you sent Me, and loved them, even as you loved Me."—John 17:23 Note 'perfected in unity.' Jesus has the power to raise the dead. Therefore all men should honor the Son just as they honor the Father. Jesus gives life to whomever he desires; divine election. The people who receive that life hear the VOICE and believe in the Father and Son

Romans 8-1: *"Therefore now no condemnation to those who are Christ Jesus who live not according to the flesh but according to the Spirit"*

This is reference to the physical resurrection from the dead whom only those who believe will experience. The unsaved will face the resurrection of judgment and eternal punishment through separation from God—the second death. Young people especially think foolishly they will never die. My first wife's best girlfriend died of a brain aneurism at the tender age of twenty-one. Hers was the first funeral we had attended. God has set the moment when we all return to him for judgment. The righteous will suffer along with the wicked because we all belong to the same human family.

Romans 10:18: *"But I say, surely they have never heard, have they? Indeed they have; Their VOICE has gone out into all the earth, and their words to the ends of the world."*

This refers to Psalm 19 that speaks to the Word of God spreading throughout the world. The Jews rejected this message even though it was made clear by the Old Testament prophets. They were a stubborn generation, but God did not cast them aside. The Word reached the Gentiles who believed. God's VOICE is loud and clear in the words, deeds, power and revelation of Jesus Christ. (John 3: 16)

The resurrection VOICE of God's Son: I Thessalonians 4:16: *"For the Lord Himself will descend from heaven with a shout, with the VOICE of the archangel and with the trumpet of God, and the dead in Christ will rise first."*

From verse thirteen forward we have the most promising and encouraging sections in the Bible. We should read it every day and memorize it. In the first part of this chapter Paul admonishes believers to stand firm in their faith. We are told how to walk the walk that pleases God. Paul says: "for this is the will of God, your sanctification."(vs.3) Then Paul moves on to the promise of hope in the resurrection of the body in vs.13ff. First there are those who have died having received Christ as Savior, this is the first death. At his coming they will be raised from death to newness of life. We who are alive rejoice with them for we all will be caught up in the air to be united with Jesus forever. "Therefore encourage one another and build up one another, just as you also are doing."(Vs.18;5:11)

Hebrews 12:26: "...and His VOICE shook the earth then, but now He has promised, saying "Yet once more I will shake not only the earth, but also the heaven."

Revelation 3:20: *"Behold, I stand at the door and knock; if anyone hears My VOICE and opens the door, I will come to him and will dine with him, and he with Me."*

These are a few of the last words in the Bible. It is as though God's VOICE is giving people their last opportunity to respond to his Word. Behold, stop and take note as something important is about to be said:

- First: Christ himself is standing at the door. We did not go seeking him but he comes seeking us. Mathew 20:28: "The Son of man did not come to be served but to serve, and to give His life a ransom for many."
- Second: He has already given his life for us; paid in full.
- Third: He stands at the door knocking on our hearts door.
- Fourth: When we hear his VOICE calling us by his Holy Spirit we are to respond, asking for forgiveness of sins and believing in him by faith.

Jesus said: "I am the way, the truth and the life, no one can come to the Father but by Me."—John 14:6 He is the only door to the kingdom. We accept his truth and obey his VOICE.

The VOICE of Reason: Revelation: 3:22: *"He who has an ear, let him hear what the Spirit says to the churches."*

In each of the seven churches John has a message for us because the churches represent in one form or another what is happening today. It is the VOICE of Jesus Christ speaking a blessing and a warning where necessary.

Chapter 2

GOD KNOWS US BEFORE WE REALIZE IT OURSELVES

Give ear and hear my VOICE, listen and hear my words — Isaiah 28:23 A profound verse.

I begin with the story of my life. I was born in Denver, Colorado at St. Luke's hospital, July 16, 1928. People talk about the "good old days" — believe me, mine were anything but good.

I am the youngest sibling of two sisters, Florence and Audrey, and one brother, Curtis. It has been told that our dad was born in Blue Jacket, Oklahoma. His great grandfather was Swedish and married a Cherokee Indian woman from the reservation. Our dad, Tony (Anthony), had black hair, brown eyes and dark skin with high cheekbones. He was six feet tall and very muscular because of the work he did. I remember my dad having eighteen-inch biceps. Our mother, Elizabeth Ann, had blue eyes, red hair and was about five feet six. So we have Cherokee, Swedish, Welch, German and English blood in our family veins. Grandma Mary Elizabeth Bouslog, my mother's mother, was an English/German mix. There could even be Irish blood in us too. It is said that German brothers came to America to settle. They had lived on the border of France and Germany. It is family lore that we have southern roots and could be related to Jefferson Davis and General Robert E. Lee.

In the late thirties and early forties I lived with my family on a small farm in Lakewood, a few miles west of Denver, Colorado, near the mountains. The drive to the farm was down long dirt roads with white wooden fences outlining a few farms here and there. Other farms had fence posts standing like sentinels held tight by several rows of barbed wire strands evenly spaced to guard cattle from breaking out and running away. One day our cow Bossy broke through a weak fence and ran off while my dad was at work and the kids were at school. When we got home we took our dog Mickey—part Collie and Shepherd—and headed down the road to search for her. Mickey found Bossy down the road flapping her tail brushing the flies off her back munching on grass.

We had pigs, chickens and two cows. We had no bathroom in the house. We used the "out house" located about fifty feet away from the house. I always was hesitant in using it because when I sat down I envisioned something biting me. We had a board walkway leading from the house to the privy to keep our feet clean and dry during the winter months. When the heavy rains came with thunder and lightning you didn't venture out. Whatever you do don't be awakened in the middle of the night with the uncontrollable urge during a snowstorm. With your pajamas on you slip on your rubber boots and throw a raincoat around your body and head for the front door. As you leave the house you grab a flashlight and point it in the direction of the potty house and trust your instincts. If the path is drifted with snow you have to shovel your way. Once on the potty hole the frigid air swirls around the outhouse and pushes its way through the knotholes and between the cracks in the boards. This is an instant freeze to your exposed butt. Then fear grips your heart and you hope you can get back to a warm bed before someone reaches out and grabs you in the dark.

I couldn't wait to get indoor plumbing.

No running water in the house meant we took turns carrying several pails of water into the house every day. The water was used for cooking, drinking and taking baths. We took our baths in a large oval cast iron tub with handles at each end. The water was heated on our coal and wood stove and then poured into the tub with cold water until the temperature was just right for jumping in. We washed our hands and brushed our teeth from a pitcher of water that was thrown outside when finished.

We had a few acres of land for grazing. For a few dollars a month my father allowed a man to graze a circus horse. He claimed his horse was very tame. One early morning I went with my dad to milk the cows. The circus horse was in the barn and had to be chased outside. I got it out of the barn. We had a slight hill beside the barn and as the horse reached the top he turned his head toward me and "WHAM," he kicked me into the side of the barn. My dad heard the thud and came running out. I was lying on the ground dazed. Fortunately when he kicked me he caught me on my right wrist and missed my head. My dad picked me up and carried me into the house. My wrist was swollen twice its size. The doctor checked me out and luckily nothing was broken. My dad called the owner and gave him one day to get the horse off our property or he would shoot it. If I turn my wrist a certain way it still cracks today.

Our dad worked for the Merchant Biscuit Company in Denver. Dad would bring home sacks of broken cookies that couldn't be sold. Audrey and I would sit on the fence and eat our bellies full. Dad threw cookies to the pigs to fatten them up for slaughter. A vivid memory I have is when I was about five or six I rode with my dad in his truck to a huge pig farm. I was instructed to stay put in the truck while dad went to talk with the owner. I got fidgety after a while and decided to find him. As I wandered I saw many stalls holding a variety of pigs. I came around a corner and suddenly I was face-to-face with a giant bore hog with tusks. He was out of his pen and headed right at me. I started running and screaming at the top of my lungs for my dad. My dad heard the commotion and came around the corner and swept me up in his arms scolding me all the while about not minding him. I didn't mind the scolding as long as I got away from that pig. That hog was going to devour me for sure.

In the evenings our dad would work as an auto mechanic. People came to trust his work and would bring their cars to him for repair. A black man named Andy worked along side my dad. If anyone tried to argue about their repairs or try to cheat my dad, Andy was right there to convince them otherwise. Andy and dad were such good friends.

My sister Audrey and I attended grammar school while Florence and Curtis attended the high school on same campus in Lakewood. The school went from K1 through K12. Florence was eight years my elder and my brother Curtis was five years older than me. My sister Audrey was one year older than me. I was the baby of the family. The large age difference between my older siblings Florence and Curtis was enough to make Audrey and me feel like we were a generation apart. After they graduated high school, Florence attended Denver University on a full scholarship and Curtis attended Colorado Teacher's College on an athletic scholarship for three sports; basketball, football and track. I envied both of them.

In grammar school I got into fights just to fight. I dared boys to try and beat me up. Some beat me but I won a few. Many days I would be sent to the principal's office where I was often spanked for flaring my temper. The worst was I typically got another whipping when I got home.

Our dad worked very hard and at times held down two jobs at once. He smoked and drank heavily at times. He always made sure there was food on the table. He and my mother got into heated arguments during his drinking spells. On several occasions they fought each other, my dad usually winning. They fought in front of their children when their tempers were out of control. Our escape was to run to our bedrooms and hide. Dad beat us with the leather strap he used to sharpen his razor. A number of times I was sent to my bed before evening meal for something I did. I would crawl into bed, get under the covers and rock my head back and forth singing a made up song to get myself to sleep. One time I got into a fight with my sister Audrey and knocked her down the back steps. She hit our snow scraper and broke her arm. I vividly remember getting the strap for that bad deed.

When I was age eight my mother got so upset with my dad's drinking that she put knives in his shirt drawer and accused him of threatening to kill her. Then she had her brother, a doctor, write up papers to put my dad away in a mental institution. It worked. One night there was a knock at the door and a sheriff stood there. He took my dad away but a few weeks later my dad's two brothers came from Missouri and got him released. There was no truth in my mother's claims but for a time we were very fearful of our father. We lived in a state of fright and fear. Not long after his arrest and release our home began to break up. Florence and Curtis left to live with friends and finish out high school. Audrey and I lived with our mother until she took off to California with a man. Grandmother heard from her a couple times and then never again.

Much later in life my sister Florence hired detectives to try and locate our mother but to no avail as so many years had passed. More years passed and after Florence died the FBI contacted me. They wanted my DNA, so I gave it to them. They thought they found what was left of my mother's body in a ditch. They think she may have been murdered. I never heard a confirmation of whether it really was my mother. This was just another sad, unsolved mystery. Sadder still, our mother never tried to find out how well we all turned out in life.

Suddenly, Audrey and I were orphans. Everyone went separate ways. We bounced around staying with our older sister Florence then to our grandmother who lived on Hooker Street in Denver. Audrey and I were moved around like a couple of pack rats from one house to another. When our dad was able to take us in we lived with him but this lasted only a short time. Our dad did hold down several jobs at one time in order to put food on the table. I remember several occasions when all we had to eat was milk toast for breakfast and beans for dinner and peanut butter sandwiches. We got well acquainted with Spam.

Audrey and I attended several schools. We moved so many times we hated going to school because each time we started a new school the subjects were more advanced than the last. We never stayed in one place long enough to have any good friends. We played musical states like some people play musical chairs. Looking back, it was amazing we learned anything at all.

For Audrey and me our dog Mickey brought us a lot of comfort. Mickey helped us forget the immediate problems facing our existence. He had beautiful coloring, red and white chest and white paws. He was very smart and he knew many tricks—lie down and roll over, bring the paper, sit up and beg for food. We loved to play hide-and-seek with Mickey. When we lived with our grandmother on Hooker Street Mickey would always sit beside me when I played marbles. One day Mickey took off to chase a mean dog that lived across the street. Just as he hit the street a Budweiser truck hit him and threw him high in the air. He yelped and came down with a thud. I jumped up and ran screaming "YOU KILLED MY DOG, YOU KILLED MY DOG!" Mickey crawled to the edge of the curb. He whimpered a few times, looked up at me and died in my arms. I carried him to the back of the house and laid him down in our garage on the dirt floor.

Each day after school I would go to the garage hoping to see Mickey alive again. A few days passed and the S.P.C.A. took Mickey away. He was truly my best friend. He filled in the missing gaps in our lives.

Here is where God stepped in. My Grandmother attended the Baptist church a few blocks away from her home in Denver. She began taking me to church with her. On one occasion she had me meet the pastor. He talked to me about Christ and the need for me to be baptized. A week or so passed and I was baptized. That baptism made my Grandmother very happy. God seemed to have his hand on my life… but for what purpose?

Chapter 3

THE HANDY WORK OF GOD

In July 1944 my dad, Audrey and I moved to Hayward, California. My dad got a job in Tracy, California as a foreman in charge of installing sprinkler systems in four major warehouses being used during WWII. Audrey and I attended Hayward High School; Audrey as a junior and me as a freshman. (I was a year behind because I had missed a lot of school due to illness.) It was a beautiful campus and had received national recognition for its design. I didn't like studying and I didn't care about grades. My teachers were very understanding and sympathetic. My father picked out most of my studies as he had visions of me becoming a doctor.

I settled into Hayward High and enjoyed being with friends who liked me for being myself. Three of my buddies are still my best friends thirty plus years later. I met and dated a number of girls during this time. I would walk several miles home with a few of them because I wasn't allowed to have a car. We took the bus on dates to the movies.

At this time our dad dated women he met at different places he frequented and would invite them to go to Reno to spend the weekend gambling. For us it was a miserable life. We yearned to run away. In fact, Audrey did run away twice. In her senior year she met a sailor at a dance in Oakland and ran off to marry him. She lived a troubled life for many years. Only her faith in God kept her life from falling apart. Later she found real happiness in a second marriage to James Owens.

But back to Hayward High and the handy work of God. In my sophomore year in high school I made a few friends. One of my buddies invited me to go with him to a dance one weekend. The place was jumping with music, laughter and dancing. The carpets had been rolled back and the hardwood floor glistened with a sparkly stuff they put on it to make the floor slick. The party had been going on for a while and drinking beer and vodka had already begun to take effect. After awhile I decided I needed some fresh air and went outside. Another girl followed. We talked about school and life in general. Her name was Dorothy Mae Dyer and she was going to change my life.

When the dance ended people began leaving and she asked my buddy if he would give her a ride home. He said yes. On the way home she sat in the back seat next to me. When we got to her place—on Oak Street just two blocks off Foothill Boulevard in Hayward—I got out of the car and walked up the long driveway to the back door of the house. We said good night. Back in the car I told my buddies this was the girl I was going to marry. They burst out laughing and challenged me to try to get a date

Dorothy Mae Dyer

with her. My buddies thought it was a mission impossible as Dorothy was a junior and very popular.

The next week at school I was determined to ask her for a date. During the lunch hour the students sat out on the front lawn of the school. Dorothy always ran around with three other girls and was seldom alone. I waited until she got up to do something and I ran to her and asked if she would go out with me. She said she would think about it. A few days later we met in the hall next to our lockers and I asked her again and she said yes. My buddies couldn't believe it because they knew she was very particular. The following weekend we went to a movie in down town Hayward. After the movie was over we stopped at the local soda shop for a milk shake then I walked her home. I tried to date other girls but always went back to Dorothy. She took parts in the high school plays and I would wait for her to finish and walk her home. This went on for several months. When we started going 'steady' my buddies had to eat crow. I did a lot of walking back and forth from school to her house so we could be together. I think I wore out a pair of shoes.

After dating a few times Dorothy decided it was time for me to meet her parents. At her home I met Mr. and Mrs. Dyer (L.P.(officially Little Pat and Willy Mae) and Dorothy's three older brothers. Her brothers, Russ, Gene and Hank, greeted me with skepticism at first but as time passed they accepted me. The two older brothers Gene and Russell were already out of school and working. Hank was in his senior year. Then a wonderful thing happened to me—the Dyers took me under their wing and accepted me as part of their family. For the first time in my life I felt like I belonged to a real family. The Dyer family replaced my father and mother. They treated me like I was one of their own sons.

At this point in my life, being part of the Dyers, I no longer worried what my father did with his life. What I most cared about was we were coming to the end of the school year, Dorothy was a year ahead of me, and I didn't want to lose her. One weekend I borrowed a car and took her for a ride up in the Hayward Hills. I asked her to marry me and wait for the right time for a wedding.

She said YES! We kissed. I was not a Christian at this time but I was still the happiest man in the world. As I look back on this time in my life I see the hand of God at work. It was truly the handy work of God making it all happen.

The summer of my junior year of high school my dad had to move to Portland, Oregon for his next job. I was almost seventeen and worked with him and made extra money. We lived in a motel room and ate out. He still found women to date. They found my dad attractive and friendly and he took care of them. This was not the kind of life I had envisioned for myself. I had a gnawing feeling God had something else for me to do. I needed to get away from my father and his lifestyle and get back to Dorothy and her loving family. I don't hold this time in my life against my dad because he was only doing what came naturally for him, divorced single and needing love. He was never the same after our mom left.

I decided I had enough of my father's lifestyle and decided to call the Dyer's to ask if I could come back to live with them. Thankfully they said yes. One day my dad left to run an errand for his company and would be gone for a couple days. That was my chance to get away. I make it to the train depot, purchased my ticket with the bucks saved from working and was on the train headed out of Portland for Hayward before my dad knew I had left. When my dad got back to the motel I was long gone. By now he was aware of where I would go.

When I arrived in Hayward I called Dorothy and she and her Dad picked me up. Her parents were more caring to me than my real parents. They gave me their spare bedroom and I settled in. Dorothy and I were together again and that was all that mattered. I would face my dad later. I stayed with the Dyer's and turned seventeen that summer. Dorothy's folks and I discussed what my next move might be and it was decided I should enlist in the service.

September 14th, '46 Dorothy and I went to the recruiting office and I signed up with the Army Air Force. One day shortly after I enlisted my dad drove into the Dyer's driveway and asked to see me. I asked Dorothy's Dad to go with me to talk with my father. My dad asked me to go back to Portland with him. I said no. I told him I had enlisted and was going to ship out soon for boot camp. He looked very surprised and then told me I was on my own from here on out. How strange for him to say that as I had been on my own almost all the time. I knew he didn't dare say anything against the Dyer's or try to pull me away from them. It was too late.

Soon I shipped off to boot camp with twenty-five other raw recruits to Camp Beal, California. I was only seventeen so I lied about my age. For some reason they did not detect this until it was too late. During the six weeks of training we learned how to handle four types of guns, work in K.P. and go on endless hikes with full equipment on. When this stint was over I was transferred to an airbase in San Antonio for more schooling.

Our barracks was another story. One night I wanted to read but the light bulb was burned out. I took a bulb from another room I mistakenly thought was vacant. Ouch, I was wrong. It turned out to be my Sergeant's room and when he returned and tried to turn on the light he was furious that the bulb was missing. Thinking there was nothing wrong in borrowing the light I said

I took it. Immediately the Sergeant dressed me down and ordered me to report to the Squadron Commander the next morning. You would have thought I had robbed Fort Knox.

The C.O.'s punishment was designed to make an example of me. He even threatened me with a court martial. I was a young raw recruit scared out of my mind. His punishment for me was to stand at attention in the blistering sun. Fifteen minutes went by. Thirty minutes went by. My uniform was wet from perspiration running down my back. The temperature was 110 degrees! Even though I felt faint I was determined to stand my ground. Suddenly a vehicle approached with flags flying on the front fender. It could only mean the Base Commander or a very high-ranking officer inside. The vehicle passed by and then screeched to a stop. Out walked the Base Commander in full dress uniform with a chest full of medals. The first thing that came to mind was "Oh boy, I am in real trouble now."

The Base Commander asked "What is your name boy and why are you standing out here in this terrific heat?" I replied, "Private Gordon K. Davis, 19256430 Sir, and I am here at the request of my commanding officer." I then shared my side of the story. He turned and entered the office and I could hear everyone inside shouting "ATTENTION." I heard voices as my Sergeant and the C.O. tried to explain their reasons for my standing in the unbearable heat. The Commander let forth a barrage of words not pleasing to the officers. Then the Commander told them to release me immediately to return to my barracks and for them to appear before him at 0900 the next morning. I got back to the barracks, stripped down and jumped into the shower. The cold water poured over me for a long, long time.

I heard a few days later through the grapevine that the C.O. and my Sergeant were transferred out of the squadron. I never heard of them again. A few months later in my career I worked in the Provost Marshall's office. Here I prepared papers for those men who were actually being court-martialed for various activities unbecoming a soldier. There never was anyone discharged for borrowing a light bulb.

What was the irony of this experience? Approximately two years later I was responsible for inspecting barracks and wouldn't you know it...replacing light bulbs.

After San Antonio it was on to Geiger Field, Washington. While there I took the USAFE courses and passed my GED test. (I later was able to graduate with my high school class in 1946) I was transferred to Cheyenne, Wyoming where I served my full term of military service. Cheyenne was truly a one- horse town with a couple grocery stores, one hotel and many bars. The biggest entertainment was the week of the Cheyenne Frontier Days Rodeo. The town was packed, bars overflowing with cowboys.

Determined to advance myself while in the service, I became office clerk for our squadron. Then I got a chance to work in our squadron supply and took it. The base had monthly inspections and my supply room was white glove spotless with everything in its proper place, shoes and clothing in their bins. I won citations every time. The Major in base supply appreciated my work so I requested to transfer to his unit where I served out my term. I reached the rank of Sergeant.

While serving my time in the Army Air Force I continued taking college courses to improve my mental skills. Dorothy and I wrote to each other of our dreams for our life ahead. When I turned nineteen I got a two-week pass and went home to the Dyer's. Dorothy and I were married by a Methodist minister whose last name was Ironmunger. He wore heavy glasses and had a look that would kill a horse. During the ceremony as we listened to Ironmunger I began to break up. Soon Barbara O'Brian, Dorothy's bridesmaid, started laughing under

Dorothy and Gordon

her breath and then Dorothy chimed in. Then my best man Ralph Hakansen joined in. We were terrible. It was emotional stress I guess. Finally we composed ourselves and Ironmunger finished the ceremony. He didn't crack a smile. We thanked him, paid him and got out of there. There were those who thought there was not much hope for the marriage because of our youth. I'm sure Minister Ironmunger questioned our sincerity. Dorothy and I took off for Santa Cruz for a two-day honeymoon and twenty-five years building a life together.

Also during this time we attended the Oakland Neighborhood Church with Dorothy's mother Willy Mae. One evening at the end of the service the invitation was given to the congregation to receive Christ. Dorothy and I went forward. Soon we were baptized. This marked a very important time in our lives. From that moment on Christ played a major role in our decision-making.

I was promoted to Corporal and could afford to bring my wife to live with me in Wyoming. In December 1948 Dorothy took the train from Hayward to Cheyenne and I went to greet her in a snowstorm. This was her first big life experience with being in snow. She was a beautiful sight.

Living together in Cheyenne was a real adventure. Our one room living quarters was an experience to remember. As I write I can see it vividly—it had a fold away bed, a china cabinet for dishes, a small two-burner stove in one corner of the room with a tassel-shade on the window. There was no refrigerator, just a wooden box that hung out the window for holding our milk and meat in the winter. It was very small but we were very happy being together.

One afternoon we decided to go to the theater down the street. We went in, sat down and noticed not many people were there. We wondered why. We watched the newsreel and then the two movies for the typical for the times price of one. Three hours later when the movie was over we got up to leave the theater and went outside. There was our answer. It was already snowing very hard and a few cars were left in the middle of the street abandoned. We ran as fast as we could to get back to our room. It was only 4 blocks away but it seemed like miles. The sleet and snow was already two feet deep and drifting. We finally reached the house with our faces almost frozen. This was January 1949. It was one of those fifty-year blizzards. Drifts of snow piled high up to thirty feet in places. It came down for two days. We got word on the radio that any army people off base were to stay put. Do not try to get back to the base. So we huddled happily in our little room for three days before we could get out. Airlifts were called in to try and get hay to the stranded cattle.

In July 1949 I received my honorable discharge papers and Dorothy and I took the train to Denver where my grandmother lived. A friend of hers had a 1929 Model A Ford up on blocks in her garage. We fell in love with this four-door sedan. It was a two-toned olive green beauty with Mohawk upholstery complete with tasseled window shades. She had only 19,000 miles and the paint on the engine blocked wasn't even burned off. Originally it had cost $800. As I recall we paid $400—a sweet deal. We headed back home to Hayward. Chugging over the Donner Pass we saw new cars stalled overheated on the side of the road, but out Model A never had to stop. We kept the Ford for two more years. Sold it with 49,000 miles on her. What a great car!

One story I have to tell you is about Dorothy. In one house we lived in the landlady was always poking her head into see what we were doing or to make sure we kept the place spotless. Sometimes it was embarrassing as she caught us in our nightclothes or no clothes at all. Dorothy was always very clean and careful. She made sure the bathroom was always perfect after we used it but the landlord lady still accused us of being untidy. Well, on the day we packed our things and were set to get out of there I loaded our things but Dorothy said wait a minute as she had one last thing to do. She went inside, took a roll of toilet paper and let it fly. She unrolled it all over the apartment and into the bathroom and all over the floor. She came out and said: "She thinks we are untidy so I let her know what I think of her constant remarks about it." We laughed all the way down the street and out of town.

Chapter 4

GOD'S VOICE: CALLED TO SERVE

B ack in California we entered a new phase of life by committing our lives to Christ. We started attending the Oakland Neighborhood Church along with Dorothy's mother who was a member. After a few weeks of listening and enjoying pastor Earl's sermons we went forward one evening and accepted Jesus Christ. Another week or so we were baptized by immersion, automatically becoming members of the church. I was already working as a tool and die engineer. My chief engineer was Mr. Nonamaker who had a big influence on my life as he also attended the Neighborhood Church. He became like a father to me on the job.

Dorothy and I became very interested in studying the Bible and taking all the classes that were offered at the time. We even took correspondent courses with Moody Bible Institute. The pastor at Neighborhood Church, Earl Sexauer, noticed our enthusiasm and interest in the church ministry. We attended the young adult Bible study taught by pastor, Reverend Earl's wife Pauline. She was an excellent teacher and we became very close friends.

I got more involved in the ministries of the church and was elected to the church board and served as an officer in the Sunday school. After serving the church and pastor a few months I was asked to accept the Challenge Hour Ministry for young married couples on Sunday evenings. We had our mini-service for the couples and then we all attended the main evening service. We averaged about forty-to-fifty folks in our group. I wrote out my little sermon and then would go out into the hills of Hayward and preach to the cows. I got lots of MOOOOOOOs.

Dorothy and I organized a calling ministry on Sunday afternoons during the summer. This work was supposed to help build the Sunday services in the Fall. When the Fall ministry began the church was filled to capacity. Our canvassing work was successful and it was a joy to be a part of what was happening in the church. People were being saved every Sunday. The church outgrew its boundaries. The Lord blessed the work we were doing. This church later moved to Castro Valley and is call the Cathedral at the Crossroads. The Lord impressed Dorothy and I with the life and work of the church.

Reverend Earl Sexauer had a vision whereby young men would be trained for the ministry and then be sent out to start satellite churches from the mother church. Before his dream could be realized Earl died of a heart attack at age forty. Before Earl's untimely passing we had several meetings discussing my interest in full time ministry. It was becoming clear to me that God was moving us in this direction. At one of these meetings he asked me point blank, "What makes you think you can preach?" I said: "I do know that if God is calling me he will provide the training opportunities for me to succeed." Then Earl asked what Dorothy thought of my decision. We had just put a down payment on a new home. I had job security and benefits making $600 a month at Friden Calculating Machine Company. Was she willing to give this up? Earl said that unless God called Dorothy it would not be wise to pursue my plan. We agreed to pray that God would call her without any prodding from either of us. I went on working at my job and studied at Bible school at night.

Several weeks passed and then early one morning Dorothy got up, took a shower and dressed like she was going out. I asked her where she was going. "If God has called you to become a minister I have to get a job so you can go to Bible college." That was the answer Earl and I had waited for. God does direct our lives if we will be patient and let him lead the way.

After Earl died the church board brought in Jacob Belig as pastor. He and Earl had been classmates in college and good friends. The church continued to grow even though Jacob was a better administrator than a preacher. He was a Stanford grad with a Masters degree in history. He did an excellent job of surrounding himself with able associates. He was the opposite of Earl in his vision for the church. Jake did not want to create new satellite churches. He knew of my plans to become a minister and encouraged me to stay and help him in this church's ministry. When I told him of our plans to start a church in San Francisco he told me it would never work. He declared we would be going to the toughest place on earth to start a church and we were not to expect any support from his church as all the money was needed to keep it going. I never asked for any support after that meeting. I knew that if God called us he would provide for our every need.

Dorothy and I entered the crossroads of our lives together by faith. Our weekends were taken up with travels across the bay to San Francisco. We were looking for a building that would be suitable to start a church. We met with other pastors in the area and only one was encouraging. All the others thought we were crazy. They said San Fran didn't need more churches.

One weekend we spotted a building on the west side of San Francisco on the corner of West Portal and Portola Drive. It was vacant and looked like the right place to begin. We contacted the owner and shared with him that we wanted to start a church. He was elated, gave us a lease and cut the monthly rent down to $500. We used all of our savings getting the place ready for services. We purchased fifty metal chairs, curtains and built a platform for the pulpit to rest upon. A dear friend gave us a hand-made pulpit with a cross in the center. We had crosses made to hang in front of the building and made a large sign: The Neighborhood Church.

One June 12, 1955 we officially opened the doors for the first service. Dorothy and I were 26 years old. I was so sure we would fill the place that I ordered another fifty chairs and spread them out in the room just off the main sanctuary. Sunday morning came and the doors opened for the first service. Ten people showed up. I went ahead and preached as if the place was packed. After the service I cried. *How could the Lord do this to us? What did we do to deserve this?* I asked the Lord to send fifteen people to the evening service or I would consider that he did not want us there.

We had exactly fifteen people that night. I should have asked for fifty. Dorothy and I spent thirteen years of our life ministering to the people of San Francisco. Our years at the Neighborhood Church were some of the happiest years of Dorothy's and my life. We have many friends that are so special from this life experience. I am thankful to God for all those who came to believe in Christ through our ministry there. The church is still there after these many years.

Dorothy and I did a lot of growing up in the church together. As I look back on those early years I am amazed that we were so bold as to think God was going to give greenhorns a house full. Dorothy and I learned the Bible together, studied together and everything I learned in college I passed on to her. And I developed my sermon ministry to the point that almost every Sunday I was hitting the mark I had set for myself. Our flock was fed on a regular diet of God's Bible. I tried my best to give them the whole council of God encompassing the whole book.

We had a servicemen's center at the church. God used this ministry to reach out to Navy, Army, Marines and Air Force people who had nothing else to do on weekends but to wander the streets of San Fran. We wore out our new Chevy bringing folks back and forth to the church for fun, refreshments and entertainment. After the games and singing I delivered the sermon. One memorable evening thirteen young men stood up and accepted Christ.

Life rolls quickly by. Dorothy and I had one son we named Dyer Gordon Davis. Dyer was the light of our life and a great son today. He was going on twelve when his Mom died. This was a heart wrenching period in our life. My son Dyer and I had to keep going on. I had to return to the business world after pastoring two churches covering twenty-one years. My professor in seminary told us that if we ever had to leave the ministry to consider the insurance business because we had a love for people. My agent was with State Farm Insurance Co, so I talked to him to see if this was a good career for me. I become an agent and worked for State Farm for thirty-seven years. During this span of years I had major heart bypass surgery at age 78 and bleeding ulcers two years later. The ulcer attack is a story in itself of how God stopped the bleeding and healed my stomach in the presence of Dr. Rosenberg, who was at first a skeptic and then a witness to the miracle of divine healing and the power of prayer.

God provided me a second major blessing to my life when he brought my second wife Sharon and I together. Magically Sharon was waiting to be by my side and help me recover and begin the second phase of my life. The life of Christ and the guidance of the Holy Spirit have been with me through it all. Isaiah 40:31 says: "They that wait upon the Lord will renew their strength, they will mount up with wings as eagles, they will walk and not be weary, they will run and not faint. Faithful is He that calls you."

Chapter 5

BUILDING LIFELONG RELATIONSHIPS

P lease stop what you are doing right now and take a moment to think along this line: God's VOICE is talking to you personally, through his word. It is his revelation. People outside the Bible will never know who God is. They will never understand why God had to send his only begotten Son to die on the cross for their sins. It is a mystery. Why would God send his Son to save the world if it could be saved any other way? In John 3:16,17 are verses we all seem to know by heart or hear repeated in Sunday school: "For God so loved the world that He gave His only begotten Son, that whosoever believes in him should not perish, but have everlasting life." God sent his Son NOT into the world to condemn the world; but that the world through him might be saved.

In my early twenties I realized God knew all about me and was playing a major role in reshaping my life according to his will. I continued to study the Bible. As I read through the Old Testament and then the New

Testament it became clearer to me how God speaks directly to us. His VOICE rings out in our ears and challenges our conscience to respond. This is true when we take the time to memorize certain passages of scripture by repeating them over and over again. We hear his VOICE speaking through the presence and power of the Holy Spirit. It is for these reasons and many more that I intend to show that the Bible is *More Than Just Words* printed on pages in a book bound with a leather binding. God speaks to me and you every day.

Realize the Bible is God's VOICE speaking to us if we only will let him be heard. First there is God's love for the world. This means he put forth a plan to save the world. Man could not save himself by himself. He was not capable since he was born in sin. Second, being a righteous judge God sent his Son to do what man could not do—to take on our sin and die on the cross to satisfy God's righteous requirement for sin. The world through God can be saved. But there is a condition most people forget or fail to understand. Jesus Christ is the only way to the Father. Jesus said, "No man can come to the Father except by me."—John 14:6

Let me try to explain the truth about God's voice. Think about when you meet someone for the first time. You may be impressed with the way that person speaks, the way he/she seems to grab your attention, the tone of their voice. You want to hear more and decide to meet again at a Starbucks for coffee. You meet again and once more you are impressed and attentive. Then you want to get to know that person more personally and you decide to meet for lunch or dinner. I am sure you have had this friendship building experience. After a while certain people strongly connect with and grow on you.

It takes time to create the friendship of a lifetime. We all have had this experience of certain people we know who have grown on us to the extent that we develop a life-long bond with them. It has happened in my life. During the time I was a pastor of my first church a couple stood out, Angelo and Corrine Rebizzo. They helped us in our ministry for many years and we spent many meaningful times together. They became a part of our family. We became life long friends. The Rebizzos became godparents to our son Dyer. After my thirteen years ministry in San Francisco was finished we continued to remain friends forever. Angelo was by my side when we buried my first wife, Dorothy. Angelo is with the Lord today.

When we moved on to our next ministry of eight years Don and Kay Bennett became our new friends. They became the godparents of our children, Curtis and Joy. We go visit them in California every year and stay for a few weeks. After I left the ministry to work for State Farm Insurance Co, we enjoyed Howard and Chris Redman. Howard was the choir director at the San Francisco Covenant church. They remain our friends to this day though many miles separate us. This represents three couples God brought our way to have fellowship and fun together creating lasting memories. Howard and I played golf every Thursday at the Olympic Club for several years, as clergy was free on that day.

Dorothy's entire family, her brothers, their wives and children, has all been a source of wonderful relationships. Dorothy's youngest brother Hank and his wonderful wife Lee created a housing development in Swansborough

Country in the mountains close to Placerville, California. Beautiful tall pined land adjacent to the Tahoe National Forrest. Hank had met a man named Swaney who sold him the land and the original farmhouse filled with antiques. Hank and Lee moved from city life to high in the mountains. We spent several glorious summers hiking and winters sharing stories, laughs and enjoying Lee's chocolate cake around their kitchen table. With vision and backbreaking work Hank and Lee with their three children, Denise, Debbie and Rick, built a hugely successful luxury housing development. Each property had about three acres of land. Today it is being cared for by one of their daughters, Debbie and her husband Rusty Harris. They live there and run the real estate business.

Dorothy's brother Gene and his wife Bunny had two children, Vickie and Kurt. Dorothy and I fell in love with Vickie. Once we took her to the Barnum and Bailey Circus. This little blond four year old just sat there and said not a peep. We were convinced she was bored but when her Grandmother asked how she liked the circus she proceeded to tell her about everything she saw. We were amazed. As the years passed Vickie adopted me as her favorite uncle. (Of course I had a lot to do with it.) And this relationship has remained strong through the years.

Lasting relationships are a blessing of God, enriching our lives over and over again. As an old song says, "getting to know all about you." We learn to love and listen to each other's voice. Are you ready and willing to give God this kind of time? God wants to lead you along with your hand in his. His Spirit will be your guide. He never breaks a promise. God's word is waiting for you to pick it up and dare to read it. At first you may find God's word is like a foreign language and it certainly is to the uninitiated. Years ago I felt that way myself. The Bible was never taught in my home. It wasn't until I reached my twenties and was invited to church that I became aware that God had a book where I could read about him. Until then he was at a great distance to me.

Since those early years of uncertainty I have spent my lifetime getting to know all about the ways God manifests himself and his Son, Jesus Christ and the Holy Spirit. The Bible is God's revelation concerning his activities and actions with man since creation. He is God who loves me. He reveals the power and purpose in sending his only begotten Son, Jesus Christ who gave himself for me that I might have peace, joy here and now and live with him forever in eternity. It took me a long time to experience this knowledge and understanding in God's word. His VOICE speaks to us today. I pray you will give yourself the time to discover this same wonderful truth. Here are a few of the timeless truths I have discovered.

Chapter 6

IN THE BEGINNING

I n the beginning man was not there, he was only a
thought in the mind of God, a possibility. Before the
universe came into existence God was there. The planets,
the stars, the solar system came forth at the sound of
God's VOICE. It was all created for his pleasure and
glory. Everything necessary for life forms was part of
the process of creation. We read about it in Genesis and
in the Psalms. "Darkness was turned into day. Therefore
all things in heaven and on earth belong to God and are
accountable to Him. He is sovereign"—Genesis 1:1ff
and Psalm 139.

In Genesis 1:1 we read: "In the beginning God..."
and what a beginning! This is the first book of five
books called The Pentateuch. From Bible scholar John
MacArther's *Bible Commentary* we learn "Genesis ends
almost three hundred years before Moses was born and
after the Exodus." Both testaments ascribe the author-
ship to Moses. Biblical scholars agree that Moses is the
writer, but it was God by his Holy Spirit who inspired
him to write it down for future generations.

Moses, scriptures say, was a baby found along the Nile in the bulrushes of Egypt, taken into Pharaoh's palace and raised to become a distinguished leader. Moses was highly educated and raised as a member of the Pharaoh's family. One day he catches one of the palace guards beating a Hebrew slave who was making bricks with mud and straw. An enraged Moses killed the Pharaoh's guard for this act of cruelty. When a surrogate mother produced the Hebrew blanket that Moses was wrapped in as an abandoned infant he was found unworthy of the royal family and banished to the desert.

For forty days and forty nights Moses wanders in the wilderness. Then God speaks personally to Moses. This is one of the most beautiful and powerful conversations in the Bible between Moses and his God. Why, because it is a classic example of God and man conversing together. Moses is minding his business out in the fields tending the sheep belonging to Jethro, his father-in-law, priest of Median, on the west side of the mountain. Moses has two of his shepherd dogs with him, well trained in handling and driving sheep. Suddenly, out of the silence of the night he hears a crackling sound. He turns and sees there is a bush burning on the mountainside but it is not being consumed by fire. His curiosity compels him to investigate. As he gets near he hears a VOICE. God was waiting for him. Take note, it was not until Moses turned aside to examine the bush that he found God is there waiting for him. Perhaps this incident should say something to us—when we are willing to stop all our foolish business of pleasing ourselves we too will find the Lord waiting to speak to us. "Be still and know that I AM God."—Psalm 46:10

Here we witness the God of creation (God's VOICE) speaking person to person with his servant Moses. For years the Jewish people have been under the bondage of the Pharaoh. God has heard their cry for deliverance. It is time to send Moses to get them out of there and return to them to their own land. Moses' past experience haunts his soul. To go back meant certain death. This is the Moses who was educated and trained in Pharaoh's court. God speaks again to Moses. His VOICE is clear: "I will certainly be with you." Moses asks God again: "What shall I tell them?" God replies, "…tell them the God of your fathers, Abraham, Issac and Jacob has sent me to you. When they say "What is His name?" Tell them I AM that I AM has sent you, this is My name forever." Here Moses had his epiphany—meeting God face to face. He received his marching orders to return to Egypt. (Genesis 3:14,15)

Chapter 7

YESTERDAY AND TODAY HE SPEAKS

E ven with an all-powerful epiphany Moses still questions God. He asks: "How can I go back since I killed an Egyptian soldier who was beating a Hebrew slave?" Moses needed strong proof for his safety from God. This conversation with God is so revealing. Moses boldly asks God to reveal himself for reassurance. Moses says: "… show me your glory." God responds, "You cannot see me face to face, for no man can see me and live. Nevertheless I will reveal my glory to you." So God took Moses and put him in the cleft of the rock, and then He covered him with His hand as He passed by." Moses was only allowed to see his God. Then God had Moses hide behind a big rock and with the brightness of God's glory he passed by the rock. The brightness of God's glory blinded Moses.

Moses, the Hebrew writer, never questioned God's existence. God always was eternally past and present. He shows us that God created heaven and earth out of nothing (ex-nihilo), which means there was only the mind of God. Since he is God he could have created to his heart's desire. So why did he create heaven and earth and put man on it? He did it to glorify his name. "God by willful act and divine word" spoke (His VOICE) all creation into existence, furnished it, and finally breathed life into a lump of dirt called man. In the same way God breathed life into all the animals on land, in the sky and in the sea. God's breath is like the mighty wind. He told Nicodemus the wind blows wherever it chooses, you hear the sound thereof but cannot tell where it came from and where it is going next, so is everyone born of the Spirit."—John 3:8. The brilliant Nicodemus replied, "How can this be?" This can be said about people who can't understand how God can communicate his voice to those who are willing to study and listen to his word in the Bible. It is God's voice. Remember it is his Word. "Oh precious is God's presence in the sight of men."

Chapter 8

THE SAME WORD OF GOD
SPEAKS TODAY

Over 2,000 years have passed since the birth of Jesus Christ and his words are as alive as the air we breathe. The Bible remains on bestseller lists. Longer than any other book in history. This is no accident. He sent his Holy Spirit to us. God existed "a priori" outside the realm of his creation. Behind God's spoken Word is God the Father, God the Son and God the Holy Spirit. God's VOICE speaks the first Word, Genesis and God's VOICE speaks the last Word, Revelation, "I AM the first and the last."—Revelation 22:13 The Trinity has a personality. Each person of the Trinity is actively involved in making himself known to man in the fulfillment of God's divine plan. As Dr. Oliver Blauser, Christian scholar and minister said, "Here we see the three faces of God."

Looking from a position outside the Trinity is complex. God is infinite, the eternal Almighty. And, we as humans are finite. He is omniscient, omnipresent and all-powerful. God the Father is Creator of all things including the universe, the heavens and the earth and everything in and upon the earth. Jesus Christ is God's only begotten Son who came to earth, born of a woman, conceived by the Holy Spirit to become a substitute for man's disobedience in the Garden rejecting God's laws and righteousness. Man cannot save himself since all have sinned and fallen short of the righteousness of God. Jesus Christ became sin for us who knew no sin that we might be reconciled to God. Jesus Christ and the Father sent His Holy Spirit to convict the world of sin, righteousness and judgment. John 16:8-11:

"Of sin, because men do not believe in Me; of righteousness, because I AM going to the Father, where you can see Me no longer; of Judgment because the prince of this world now stands condemned."

There is the righteous law of God that decrees that every person born of a woman is born in sin following the curse of Adam and Eve. You had nothing to do with being born and I had nothing to do with my being born. Yet, God's righteous judgment must be satisfied for he cannot look upon sin. There is no way one can save himself in the eyes of God. The Bible says "ALL SINNED." God did not choose to leave us orphans without hope. He sent his only begotten Son to become sin for us that we might become the righteousness of God. Jesus Christ became sin for us (took our sins in his body on the tree) "Because of his sacrifice we live and breathe new life, a new creature in Him."—II Corinthians 5:21

As I write these words I am reminded there are those who have not been exposed to the Bible and may not fully understand what we are talking about when we say one must be born again, because there are those who believe all God wants is a life lived serving others and obeying the golden rule to do unto others as you would like others to treat you. Please let me explain. The Bible says every person must be saved on the basis of having received Jesus Christ into their hearts by faith. Jesus said to his disciples: " I am the way, the truth and the life, no one can come to the Father except he believes in me."— John 14:6. You cannot come up to God any other way. All the 'good works won't do it. All our works are as filthy rags in God's sight. No one is good enough. Even mother Teresa with all her wonderful missionary work saving lives. Setting the highest standard of 'doing good' is for naught without the saving faith in Jesus Christ. Jesus made this very clear in his encounter with Nicodemus, ruler of the Jews in John 3:3ff: "You must be born again." This is called the second birth.

Following salvation every born again Christian receives the Holy Spirit by faith and trust on the promises of God's word.(John3:3f) His word is truth and He cannot not lie.(John 14). Therefore we understand and believe that the entire Trinity is involved in the Christian walk of faith. They are co-existent, co-equal and co-eternal. Jesus said: "I can do nothing except what I see My Father do and I do only those things that are pleasing in His sight." (John 5:19) The Holy Spirit does whatever the Father and the Son tell Him to do.

In the great Old Testament story we catch the first glimpse of God's presence. This is in truth the greatest story that was ever told. It is greater than the greatest novel and truer than a statement of fact because it is God's VOICE on God's authority. Exodus 20:6: "I am the Lord your God who brought you out of the Egypt, out of the land of slavery. You shall have no other gods before me."

In the wilderness experience of the people of Israel God chooses to reveal himself in a cloud during the day and a pillar of fire by night. With these visible symbols he led the children of Israel out of Egypt, through the Red Sea, through the wilderness. He provided manna when they were hungry and gave them water in the hot dry desert. He led them into the promised land of Canaan. He revealed his presence and power to Moses with the burning bush. He gave his people the Ten Commandments to teach them his laws to govern their lives. The law was given so that we can know the character and justice of God.

Following the instruction of the Ten Commandments that God gave to Moses the people experienced the phenomena of lightening, thunder and smoke and heard the trumpet. They became frightened and called out to Moses for help. Moses said to the people, "...do not be afraid. God has come to test you so that the fear of God will be with you to keep you from sinning."(Exodus 20:18-20)

What a contrast this picture is to the believer living today. Instead of God's wrath we have forgiveness of sins in his Son, Jesus Christ. Instead of fear we have hope, instead of eternal damnation we have eternal life, instead of anxiety we have peace with God, instead of doubt and uncertainty, we have the guaranteed promises of God, instead of sorrow we have joy unspeakable and full of glory, instead of rejection we have the predestined will of the Father. There is nothing that we have done to merit God' favor. All have sinned and fallen short of God's righteousness.

Chapter 9

GRACE

Here is where the GRACE of God reaches out to touch us. By grace we are saved through faith. Not by anything you have done to merit it. GRACE is God's free gift to all who believe. GRACE, GRACE, GRACE. He freely bestowed this grace on all his chosen children. Grace is one of the most powerful words in the Bible. For years biblical scholars have wrestled trying to define this word, parse it and extract its full impact. Grace can mean courteous good will when someone admits wrongdoing; or a person demonstrates all the social graces. For the Christian it speaks of the free and undeserved Grace of God in providing salvation to sinners.

Grace is finding undeserved favor with God who provides the sacrificial, substitution for the death of Jesus Christ for the world. In the Pauline Epistles there is this beautiful Greek salutation to the churches— *charis humin kai eirana apo Theou Patros*— grace to you and peace from God our Father. It is an opening greeting that inspires the person or church receiving it. Imagine what would happen if we greeted everyone this way. It produces a calming effect on our nerves.

> Romans 3:21-24:
> *"The righteousness of God through faith in Jess Christ for all those who believe; for there is no distinction; for all have sinned and fall short of the glory of God, being justified as a gift of His grace through the redemption which is in Christ Jesus."*

There are those who, having heard or read this, can't understand why it was necessary for someone to die for them? They have a hard time believing they are a sinner. The Bible says over and over again that all have sinned and fallen short of God's righteousness. All are born in sin. No one can satisfy the righteous demands of God, someone must die and pay the just requirements of God's law, and God in his great grace and mercy sent his Son to pay the full price with his blood. Without the shedding of blood there is no remission for sin. Here is that word GRACE again: "For by GRACE are you saved through faith. IT IS God's GRACE, God's grace not ours. It is FREE. "Who His own self bore our sins in His body on the tree, that we being dead to sin might live unto righteousness."—1 Peter 2:24

Chapter 10

THE APOSTOLIC COMMISSION

Why was it necessary for God to send his Apostles out into the world? Following Pentecost there were no more Apostles. Why? In *Mounce's Complete Expository Dictionary of Old & New Testament Words*, the Greek term "apostolos" means one who is sent; a messenger; a delegate to one sent as an envoy of a master. In the Gospel of Luke the word is used exclusively to designate the Twelve Apostles who were with the Lord. They were by his side as his companions. Therefore, 'Apostle' was a special designation only to the Twelve, and no one else. Certain requirements were necessary to receive this title. An Apostle had to have been with Jesus, listened to his teachings, and as such held an important place in the church.

Paul recognizes this distinction. Paul was set apart by Christ on the road to Damascus, given a special appointment to take the good news with him in each of his three missionary travels which covered many miles.(Galatians 1:17) He considered himself "the least of the apostles, one untimely born, unfit to be called an apostle, BUT by God's grace, I am what I am"—I Corinthians 15:9ff. This was not man's doing but God's grace alone. Without the leading of the Holy Spirit Paul was an empty bag of wind.

God's VOICE reaches out to touch us by sending the Holy Spirit, that is received when a person is born again. Every day the Christian needs to thank God for his graces bestowed upon his life. There is his divine election for those who are in Christ, his saving faith, his redemption of sinners, and the promise of eternal life given through all his saving grace. The Christian knows that no matter what suffering they may have to endure they are safe and secure in the grace and peace that surpasses all understanding in Christ Jesus. (Hebrews 4:1; II Corinthians 4:15). More is available on 'grace' in *Mounce's Complete Expository Dictionary of Old & New Testament Words.*

Other graces are those one receives when extra time is allowed to pay back a debt or loan. 'Grace' may refer to a closing prayer: "may the grace of our Lord be with you."—II Corinthians 13:14 Or, a prayer given before a meal is served is a grace. Paul uses this term in his Epistles by way of introduction and closing praises to God; "Grace and peace to you from God our Father and the Lord Jesus Christ." Paul constantly asked the Lord to heal him from some infirmity he had and the Lord told him "my grace is sufficient for you." When you have received God's grace you don't need anything else. It was God's grace that sent Jesus Christ to the cross, for our salvation.

Chapter 11

Missing the Mark

I n the Old Testament God's VOICE is heard as he speaks through his prophets with his message. They are in-turn to give his words to the nations. Today we begin to understand how far short we miss the mark. At this point in our story we begin with the question *Do you believe in the God of the Bible?* Even the devil knows God's VOICE, believes in God and trembles. Jesus told his disciples you believe in God, believe also in Me.(John 14) God has put eternity into every man's heart. He alone is to be worshiped. We are to love God with all our heart, soul and mind and we are to love our neighbor as we love ourselves. In the New Testament God's love is called in Greek, 'agape.' This type of love is the highest form of love. Jesus is this love. We are called upon "to love our own bodies" that is to take care of our body because "our body is the temple of God." God by his Holy Spirit is to occupy our body beside Jesus Christ.

When we come to the New Testament we see the unfolding covenant promises God gave to Moses, Abraham, Isaac and Jacob and the major and minor prophets. Further revealed is the promise of the Messiah, Jesus Christ. In the New Testament we discover who this person is, what it is he will do for all mankind. The mystery that was hidden in the Old is now revealed in the New. There are unwritten laws of the heart that are universal. God has placed them there. We understand the difference between good and evil. Unchecked we may rape a woman and kill someone we disagree with in a fit of anger, but we know innately we have broken the natural law; "thou shalt not kill." Our conscience bears witness to this fact. God promises to forgive us when we repent but the consequences of missed opportunities haunt us.

Then there are the civil laws that are instituted to help society keep from becoming brutally uncivilized. What kind of life would exist and how many of us would survive if all these laws were suddenly removed? I would hate to imagine it. Can anyone fathom the depths of the universe, or space, matter and time? Science prides itself in its vast knowledge of the universe and contemplates where and when it all began and where it will end. But there are still many mysteries yet to be discovered. God says man's wisdom is foolishness and man by his own wisdom can never know God. These mysteries challenge man and keep him probing for answers. Perhaps this too is God's intent. There is much more to the Trinity than God's truth and our imagination can fathom.

You cannot box God in on your terms. God is always working outside the box of man's scientific explorations and hypotheses. Can man with his finite mind fully understand an infinite God? No. But that does not make God less than who he is. The Trinity is God the Father,

God the Son and God the Holy Spirit. When we speak of one person we speak of them together. Jesus said I and my Father are one. God declares the wisdom of this world is foolishness in his sight, and man by his own finite wisdom (REASON) can never know God because God is Spirit and without the Spirit of God made alive in man he can never accept his truths. Without God man is a dead-man walking. He is spiritually dead. The beginning of wisdom is the fear (reverential) of God. (Proverbs 1:7). In man's fallen, distorted and confused nature he is an empty shell without God's truth and wisdom to guide him. He is "full of sound and fury, signifying nothing."

Even Pilate in Rome with all his power and authority over people asked Jesus: *What is truth?* The question really should be today *Does man want the truth?* Jesus said (his VOICE) to his disciples "I AM the way, the truth and the life, no man can come to the Father except by me."—John 14:6 My dear friend and Hebrew scholar, Dr. Oliver Blauser points out the word "TRUTH" in the Old Testament always means a PERSON. Therefore in the New Testament Jesus Christ is the truth. The beacon light of this statement shines on the cross. Without the shedding of blood there is no forgiveness of sin.

Chapter 12

THE BREATH OF GOD

I n the beginning man was not there, he was only a
thought in the mind of God, a possibility. The Psalmist
tells it like it is;

> *O Lord Thou hast searched me and known me,*
> *Thou dost know when I sit down and when I rise up,*
> *Thou dost understand my thought from afar.*
> *Thou dost scrutinize my path and my lying down,*
> *And art immediately acquainted with all my ways.*
> —Psalm 139:1-3.

Here is God's order:

Creator

"In the beginning God created the heavens and the
earth, and the earth was formless and void."—Genesis 1:1.
Before time and space there was God. Some Biblical
scholars think the world cannot be over 10,000 years old.
If this is true then God had a different way of dating the
earth. A day with the Lord is as a thousand years.

Creation

"Out of the empty void God spoke His word and everything was set in motion (ex nihilo) out of nothing. God forever existed eternally. He pre-existed in eternity past, before creation began. He is not bound by the world he created."—Genesis 1:1

Creature

"...and God formed man of the dust of the ground, breathed (the spirit) into his nostrils, and man became a living spiritual being." with a body, soul and spirit.—Genesis 2:7

In writing the Pentateuch, (first five books of the Bible—Genesis, Exodus, Leviticus, Numbers, and Deuteronomy) also called the Septuagint or Torah, Moses made no attempt to explain the existence of God or what he was like. Therefore, all things in heaven and on earth belong to God. He owns the cattle on a thousand hills and the gold and the silver are his. Man has to begin at the beginning with God. The great theologian Dietrich Bonhoeffer said man can understand the beginning only if he begins with God's Son, Jesus Christ and goes backwards to where it all began. We accept the historical revelation God gave to the early prophets by divine inspiration. We were not there but God's VOICE was there and it was powerful. "In the beginning God..."—Gen. 1:1. All truth hangs on these words.

This may seem irrelevant at first but when you realize the whole point of man's forgiveness and redemption ends with Jesus Christ then everything that God planned and did prior to this event makes sense. "He came not to be ministered unto, but to minister and give His life a ransom for many." — Mathew 20:28 He came "for us." Jesus was sent by God "for us." The whole first chapter of Ephesians is Paul's reminder to us of God's blessings of redemption in Jesus Christ. One writer makes a valid observation on Ephesians chapter one, verses three to twelve:

1:3-6 the work of the Father is Election (Romans 9:11; II Peter 1:10)

7-12 the work of the Son is Redemption (Galatians 3:13)

13-14 the work of the Holy Spirit's Protection (John 17:11)

Here is the spirit of wisdom and of revelation in the knowledge of Jesus. He personally bore our sins in his own body on the tree (He offered himself on it) that we might die to self and to sin and live to receive God's righteousness. "By His wounds you have been healed." — I Peter 2:24. Also read Psalm 103, "Bless the Lord, O my soul."

We have to go back to the beginning, with all that was accomplished before man ever looked into the starry heavens. Genesis 1:1 says: "In the beginning God created the heavens and the earth." The Psalmist put it like this, "The heavens declare, make known the glory of God, and the earth is busy displaying His handy work." To paraphrase Psalm 19:1: this is the Old Testament's declaration that God is/was there all along. From Walter Brueggemann, protestant scholar and theologian — considered one of the most influential Old Testament scholars of the last several decades—on the book of Genesis: "In creation we have God's divine fiat, out of nothing, ex nihilo, literally, there was nothing here to begin with but God. God wills what will be in the beginning and nothing can stop it. It is irreversible and cannot be nullified. The mode of that binding is SPEECH. With the sound of his VOICE he calls the world into being. By God's speech that which never was comes into being. It is God alone who authors life."

Here we see the Trinity at work. God created the heavens and the earth...then we see, and the Spirit of God was moving over the surface of the waters...and later in Genesis 1:26: "...let Us make man in our image, according to Our likeness..." The Bible starts and ends with the Trinity; the Father, the Son and the Holy Spirit. In the Old Testament Hebrew one of the words for Spirit is wind or breath. In Genesis 1:2: "This is the same moving breathing voice of the Spirit that reaches out to us today."

The breath of God (his VOICE) is still moving across the face of the earth. His breath is in your nostrils. The Psalmist cried: "...let everything that has breath praise the Lord." (Ps.150: 6) "He Himself gives to all breath and life." —Acts 27: 25 Following Jesus' resurrection he came to his disciples who were in the upper room and the doors were shut, he said: "Peace be with you, as the Father has sent Me, I also send you." And when He said this, He breathed on them and said to them, "Receive the Holy Spirit." Do you realize that it is God who gives life to all things? It is his breath that gives you life; it can be taken from you in an instant.

Most Christians don't have any trouble thinking about God and the Lord Jesus Christ. In the church pastors and teachers speak of them all the time as they should. But often something is missing. The problem is little credit is given to Jesus Christ for sending the Holy Spirit. Notice how often our prayers end with "In Jesus' name. Amen." We assume somehow that is all that needs to be said. This attitude shows what little time we have given to studying what the Scriptures say about the important role the Holy Spirit plays in our daily life, including prayer.

Chapter 13

GOD DEFINED MARRIAGE FROM THE VERY FIRST BREATH OF LIFE

God created one Adam and one Eve. They were to be a family. It is a fact that whenever society lowers itself to go contrary to God's laws that society will eventually suffer disastrous consequences, as the downfall of Rome and her history that proves it. Is America slowly moving in the same direction? A few historians and religious leaders think so. We are losing our civility and moral fiber and the family resiliency. Whenever mothers stop taking a strong stand to protect the family, society as a whole starts sliding down a slippery slope

Getting back to Genesis, I found a sovereign God provided everything necessary for the happiness of Adam and Eve. He placed them in the Garden saying, "Be fruitful and multiply and fill the earth, and subdue it, and rule over everything."—Gen. 1:28. They had responsibility not to be idle. They could not have done this without 'free will' given to them by God. When God unites a couple, one man and one woman, in marriage they receive a most wonderful gift—each other. They are to enjoy everlasting companionship.

There is nowhere in the Bible where deviant sex acts are condoned. The scriptures teach the opposite. The Israelites learned this lesson with the golden calf and later when they stopped listening to God's VOICE. Marriage is a sacred unity between a man and a woman. To say different goes against God's Word and against nature. Anyone who dares to read Romans chapter one will get the Apostle Paul's reply and he compliments what God has already said. When people deny the truth of God's Word they naturally want acceptance in society. They call Christians "bigots" who hold fast to God's word about the sanctity of marriage between a man and woman. This must mean God is also a bigot. Let them deal with God. People who are confused about their physicality need counseling from a reliable professional Christian psychologist. There is no shame in seeking such help. The Bible gives us a clear picture of what marriage can be like in the book of Ephesians. Each person compliments the other in significant ways.

We hear God's voice speaking: "…submitting yourselves one to another in the fear of God"—Ephesians 5: 21. First and foremost is the submission of the couple to the will of God. Both husband and wife have to have a clear picture of what this means. It begins with the reverential fear of God and asking him to be a partner in their lives. He has sent the Holy Spirit to be a partner with us 24/7/365. Without this initial confession there can be no moving forward. Married life has to begin under the umbrella of God's Spirit. One recognizes that there are many examples where couples have made it on their own without God. But, statistics show the presence of God in the home with a family makes all the difference in the world. Through study of God's word, prayer and taking time to listen to God's VOICE and with obedience to his will one can enjoy a thorough successful, happy life.

Marriage requires open and free communication with honesty, integrity and trust in each other. Ephesians verse 22: "...wives submitting themselves to their husbands, as unto the Lord." This is not the husband who demands this, but the Lord. Regardless of her station in society, her job, her intellect, her career, she is to willingly and lovingly let her husband take the lead. And, by the same report the husband is to not sit back and let the wife lead. His wife is his personal possession in God's sight and he sure better take care of her or he will answer to God. He is head of the wife, as Christ is head of the church (verses 23-33). "For this cause shall a man leave his father and mother, and shall be joined to his wife, and they two shall become one flesh." — Vs.31. This is more than a sexual relationship, it means they become a unified whole with each person making their important contribution to the family unit.

There must be love and respect from the very beginning of marriage. I have been reading a book entitled *Love and Respect: The Love She Desires; The Respect He Desperately Needs* by Dr. Emerson Eggerichs. I highly recommend it to all married couples and to those who are contemplating marriage. Allow me to give you just a few samples of his perspective:

"How can I get my husband to love me as much as I love him?"

Eggerichs' Answer: This was the basic question I heard from wife after wife who came to me for counseling during twenty plus years I pastored a growing congregation. The key premise is "husbands love your wives, wives respect your husbands."—Ephesians 5:25 This is a great book for a couple to read it together. When husband and wife are in love and have been married for several years they have a way of meshing together their two hearts. They can recognize each other's voice anywhere. It may be in a shopping center or just walking down the street. They call out to their spouse and are immediately recognized.

When all the above is ignored or disobeyed for NARCISTIC or SELFISH reasons the result is divorce. Their voices no longer respond in unison. I have witnessed this disaster take place with my own parents and family; lives of children are scarred forever. Couples always find excuses to defend the reason for divorce. Often one spouse does not love the other or they disagree as to who should take the lead role in the marriage. By the time the decision is made God is no longer a player. Where children are involved they always suffer loss. The majority of people who marry today never consider God's role in helping them succeed and find true happiness. Over 50% of marriages end in divorce. Why?

"What happened to put such a stain on God's gift to husband and wife? Why do so many marriages fail?"

Eggerichs' Answer: No one can point the finger at God. Every man is tempted when he is drawn away by his own lust, and when lust prevails sin is at the door. God is not the author of temptation. Here again is man's free will being exercised. (James1:13-15) God never intended marriage to end in the divorce courts.

My wife and I have been married now for thirty-eight years. As time passes she is more beautiful than ever. Our relationship continues to grow deeper. She is my dearest friend, my confidant, my soul mate. Believe me, as I watched my older brother's life unfold before me with several divorces, the grass is not greener on the other side of the broken down fence. I knew all of his wives and his first one was definitely the best. He let popularity as an athlete, pride and sex blind him. Don't get me wrong, I loved my brother dearly and practically worshiped him myself. But his lifestyle I did not care for. Many years passed before my brother finally came to Christ.

There are instances where married couples have all the money they need and they still can't get along. Money never brought true happiness. Love of God, family and friends does. Stop and think for a moment about God's love for the first couple, Adam and Eve. It is a reflection of what he can do for all of us who will let him. He gave them the breath of life and he could take it away. In his love he created them male and female. They had each other for companionship. He gave them free reign in the Garden and over the earth so they in return would be responsible caretakers of his creation. They were to rejoice in their worship of their Creator. Their workshop was the Garden. Childbearing was to be without pain. This was true paradise. They were to be a reflection of God's blessings and gift of love.

What does the word LOVE mean to you when you say it?

Let me explain the three types of love. First, there is 'erotic love' which is sexual and sensual. Second, is 'philo love' as in "I love you as a friend." Third, there is the Greek word for the highest meaning of love, 'agape love.' Jesus used 'agape love' on several occasions. An example of 'agape love' is found in John 3:16: "God so loved the world."

Adam and Eve walked and talked with God freely in the Garden. They were naked yet not ashamed. Later on they found themselves naked and became ashamed. What change happened to them physically and spiritually to make them express shame? They died within and death took its course. They were to work together as husband and wife in the Garden. Today's culture breeds the modern idea that couples don't need to work as a team. This notion is truly nonsense with God. He said that a man who does not work should not eat. When man left the Garden God said: "...you will work by the sweat of your brow and women will have pain in childbearing." The word WORK is mentioned many times in the Bible.

We want to do everything we can to help and encourage our children to be successful and be happy in life. While they are in our charge we love them and make sure they receive all our love and care and a good education and develop a life of integrity, trust, honesty and reliability. We love them and then we give them their freedom to establish a life on their own. It is their turn to make value judgments and choices that they will have to live with. We are a reflection of God's love given to them every day.

Once they fly the nest it is up to them to determine what kind of life they choose. As parents we will always be there for them. We don't stop loving them if they fall or make mistakes in judgment. In a finite way we try to do what God did in an infinite way for us. "Train up a child in the way he should go. Even when he is old he will not depart from it."—Proverbs 22:6 "Do not hold back discipline from a child..."—Proverbs 23:13 "Those whom the Lord loves He disciplines."—Hebrews 12:6.

.

Chapter 14

THE BIBLE IS NOT DEAD WOOD

T HE BIBLE IS GOD'S VOICE SPEAKING TO ALL
OF HUMANITY. It is more than just PRINTED
WORDS AND PHRASES. It is not dead wood; it is more
than phrases written in a book bound in leather. IT IS
GOD'S DIVINE REVELATION.

In the Bible we read about the many ways God seeks
to communicate with humanity. He reveals his existence
through theophany (an appearance of a god to a human);
and anthropomorphic (taking on human characteristics)
forms. He reveals his thoughts through the Holy Spirit,
the third Person of the Trinity. This becomes readily
recognizable as we go deeper and deeper into the text.
The Bible does not defend itself; it needs no defense.
The wonder of the Bible is that God is pleased to reveal
himself to us on a personal level. The Bible is not com-
plicated. It was addressed to ordinary people from all
walks of life. Its message is universal. If man chooses to
ignore God's truths he suffers certain life consequences.
Isaiah 28:23: " Give ear and hear my VOICE, listen and
hear my words."

On Friday evenings, following WWII, the late Dr. D.M. Lloyd Jones held discussion meetings in one of the halls in Westminster Chapel, England. Wars and calamities seem to have a way of waking people up. The numbers in attendance became so large because more and more people were requesting lectures on the doctrines of God. Dr. Jones had to move his sessions into larger quarters. He led these discussions about God from 1952 to 1955. These lectures are now available in tapes and on the computer (http://www.mljtrust.org). He speaks strictly from the Bible's evidence. I highly recommend them to anyone who is serious to study God.

Complex academic phraseology or theological issues do not encumber Dr. Jones' pastoral lectures. He wanted the truth to be in understandable terms for lay people. Jones wanted to minister to the heart as well as the head. His goal was to teach the fundamental doctrines of the Word of God. I have cherished a number of his books in my library, especially *The Sermon on the Mount* Studies in Matthew, Ch. 5. He made it clear at the start that the Bible is not involved in intellectual pursuits or the myriad of philosophies that abound in men's minds. "The Bible makes clear that: the wisdom of this world is foolishness with God."—I Corinthians 2:19-20 (Paul). God makes himself known by speaking his VOICE personally with different people both in the Old and New Testament.

Dr. Lloyd Jones addressed his audience with these words: "Are you anxious to find God? Are you anxious to know God? Then you must close your mind to all inferior outside thoughts, ideas and false presuppositions and come to the Bible and let it speak its truth one step at a time through progressive revelation. You shall seek Me and you will find Me if you search for Me with all your heart. We have to determine to study the Bible with an open mind, with no preconceived ideas. Let God's Word speak its truths alone. This is my whole reason for presenting this study in the Bible, that you recognize how God speaks to your heart on His own terms."

Chapter 15

GOD'S VOICE:
MORE THAN JUST WORDS.

I am trying to show that the Bible is MORE THAN JUST WORDS in a leather bound book. GOD'S VOICE IS BEHIND EVERY PAGE. It is God's voice behind, before, under every period, coma and semicolon. It is God's exclamation point. I want to quote from the well-known philosopher- theologian, Dr. Francis Schaffer's book *God Who is There; The Importance of Truth* (pgs 157,158) regarding the importance of truth. Dr. Schaffer writes: "The Scriptures are important, not because they are printed in a certain way nor bound in a certain kind of leather, nor because they helped many people. This is not the basic reason for the Scriptures being overwhelmingly important. The Bible, the historic Creeds, and orthodoxy are important because God is there, Jesus Christ is there and the Holy Spirit is there and, finally, that is the only reason they have their importance. The God who is there is of such a nature that He can be loved, and I am of such a nature that I can love...I know what man is, and I know who I am." These thoughts are taken from his Trilogy series; excellent for those who love theology.

A serious student will take the time to study the Scriptures and with more study they begin to hear God speaking to them. It carries the

authoritative and living VOICE of God. In the New Testament we have the preaching of Christ as the proclamation of the "Logos of God."(Mounce) "Man does not live by earthly bread alone, but by every word that comes from the mouth (the VOICE) of God."—Matthew 4:4, 12:37

THE BIBLE IS THE VOICE OF GOD speaking to the world. Hebrews 1:1-2:

"God, after He spoke long ago to the fathers in the prophets in many portions and in many ways, in these last days is still speaking (his VOICE) to us in His Son, whom He appointed heir of all things, His glory and the exact representation of His nature, and upholds all things by the word of His power. When He had made purification of sins, He sat down at the right hand of the Majesty on high." Amen.

Listen to the theology in these words: this is God's progressive revelation. Hebrews chapters 1 and 2:

God's VOICE spoke to us, in the prophets, (divine inspiration)
Today He speaks to us in his Son. (second person of the Trinity)
He is heir of all things, and by him the world was created, (Jesus is omnipotent, all powerful, equal with God)

He is God's radiance, the exact representation of
God's nature (the
One and the same person—co-eternal)
All things are held together by the power of his
word, (his
VOICE speaks and it is done)
He alone made purification for our sins, (only
Jesus Christ could
satisfy the Father by His death and resurrection)
He is seated in power at right hand of the Father
(he is beside God)

We need to reread this passage several times until it sinks into our heads and hearts and claim it for ourselves with shouts of joy and praise. The Hebrew writer reminds us over and over again that Jesus Christ is our High Priest and is superior to the angels, who do his bidding. He is superior to the Old Testament High Priests and their sacrifices as he became the ultimate sacrifice for sin. He was lower than the angels and then was raised from the dead and sits on the throne with the Father. (Romans 8:26) We readily accept such phrases as 'Good Housekeeping Approval' on home products and services or 'FDA Approved' on food and drugs or 'lifetime warranty' and the official New York Times best seller list. We rely on these pronouncements as though they were set in concrete. Yet when we hear that God speaks to us we question its validity as though he can't really mean it; how could this *really* be true? We call good bad and bad good according to our fabricated ideals, values and ideas. If it fits our frame of reference its okay. If it doesn't fit it must be false or not worthy of our attention.

People often get confused about who wrote the Bible and how it arrived in its present form? Some may think one or two people wrote the holy book or that it is a fictitious piece of writing created to deceive people. They wonder—how could one author be so diverse in experience throughout history? God, some believe, is a charlatan myth. They claim Jesus didn't have a real body only a spirit. With man's proclivity toward sin and disbelief it is thought to be impossible for him to write an honest historical story about God's dealings with mankind covering approximately 2,000 years in the Old Testament and 2,000 years to the coming of Jesus Christ.

In the process of writing God's story it took time for the development of God's divine revelation. First there was God's VOICE speaking to man and the oral transmission of his word through his chosen instruments, the prophets. The Pentateuch, (the first five books of the Old Testament) was given to us through Moses. Biblical scholars note this to be interesting because the book of Genesis ends 300 years before Moses was born so how could Moses have written it? It was not written until after the Exodus took place. This is another proof of divine inspiration. II Timothy 3:16: "Study to show yourself approved unto God, a workman that needeth not be ashamed, rightly dividing the words of truth."

You are not going to learn anything by hearsay or listening to those who speculate or spin falsehoods. Study God's Word. Listen to his voice. One of my spiritual leaders told me long ago that truth crushed to the ground shall rise again. No one can stop its power. Moses was one of the major players in God's plan. When you read all the instances in which Moses and God interact in the

Old Testament it is easy to see God inspired Moses to tell everything that transpired in the beginning. Its geographical setting is Mesopotamia. God brought Moses up to speed. Both the Old and New Testament ascribe the author as Moses. Genesis was written after the Exodus but before Moses' death. God used over forty different individuals over a period of 1400 to 1600 years to tell his story. They wrote down God's Word as directed by the Holy Spirit. There are many instances in the Old Testament where God spoke personally to these people. This is God's progressive revelation over 2000 years.

Therefore, the Scripture is God's BREATH and God's VOICE throughout the Bible. It is God speaking before the Bible was ever put into print. In II Timothy 3:15 we read: "Every Scripture is God breathed, given to us by divine inspiration… so that the man of God may be complete, proficient… for every good work." He spoke to the forefathers and through the prophets. These days he is still speaking through his only begotten Son, Jesus Christ. Hebrews 1:1: "Jesus Christ is the final Word" (Gk. Logos). He introduces us to the Holy Spirit that he sends us to fulfill God's plan." See John, chapters 14-17, as these can be called his spiritual promises to us.

Listen to the opening lines of the book of Hebrews 1:1-3:

"God, after He spoke (his VOICE) long ago in the fathers in the prophets and in many ways, in these last days has spoken (his VOICE) to us in His Son, whom He appointed heir of all things, through whom He made the world"

If man rejects God's pronouncement that male and female are created in his image he is confronted with a double doubt—God is not the creator and God doesn't exist. Therefore man has surrendered his right to a true and living relationship with God. He has ostracized himself from the presence and fellowship with God who is the only way, the truth and the life. He now becomes his own boss, his own god. He begins with anthropology (man) and then examines revelation from his eyes and not God's. When man denies God who created him he denies the truth God meant for him to have. His mind is filled with humanistic philosophies and ignorant pre-suppositions. The consequences of rejecting God are disastrous because there is only one correct answer; faith and trust in Jesus Christ. Paul the apostle made it clear that God will give you up to believe your lie. Doubters, agnostics and atheists blatantly deny and suppress the truth. This is the devil's lie:

> *"For they exchanged the truth of God for a lie and worshiped and served the creature rather than the Creator, who is blessed forever… and God gave them over to a depraved mind, to do those things that are not proper."* — Romans 1:24,28.

The vast majority of the world loves the idea that they do not need God, they do not need Jesus Christ and they do not need the Holy Spirit. They have autonomy and freedom to do as they please and don't like anyone messing around on their sacred turf. The past 4,000 years has revealed the disastrous results of man living without God. Choosing to say there is no God, no laws, no absolutes has resulted in chaos around the world. When man begins subjectively he begins with himself and all his thinking revolves around his humanistic, narcissistic needs, ideas and philosophy.

I have been amazed at the direction our country is going. America is slowly dying because it no longer listens to God's VOICE. A careful study of the history of Israel reveals how many times they turned their eyes away from God and the disastrous results that followed. These results are always due to the hardness of man's heart. Man's destiny is dependent upon his response to Jesus Christ. In Mark chapter 8:34-38, Jesus called the people to himself and said to them:

> *"Whoever desires to come after Me, let him deny himself, and take up his cross and follow Me. For whoever desires to save his life will lose it, but whoever loses his life for My sake and the gospel's will save it. For what will it profit a man if he gains the whole world and loses his own soul? Or what will a man give in exchange for his soul?"*

In other words, DON'T SELL OUT YOUR SOUL TO THE DEVIL!

Currently I am reading a book called *The Harbinger: The Ancient Mystery that Holds the Secret of America's Future* by Jonathan Cahn. Each chapter informs us about Israel and America in comparison from 9/11 to future engagements with life. It warns of impending judgment if America does not heed the warnings. Fifty years ago it was important that a man learns to make his own way by hard work. Because of our family situation—divorce at the age of eight—I soon learned if I was to survive I had to work very hard. My life was not a bowl of cherries. But it took me a few years to get my head straight. I hated school because I never stayed long enough in one place to enjoy it. My older sister and brother were a generation ahead of me and already in college. I had to do something. So, at seventeen I joined the Army Air Force. After my discharge from the service I began working my way through college one step at a time. I was determined to prove I could accomplish whatever I set my mind to. It is a story too long to tell but I can tell you Jesus Christ picked up my life and set me on solid rock. I looked to the Lord to give me wisdom and understanding so I would make as few mistakes as possible. I lost my father and mother and found another wonderful family in my wife's parents. The Dyer's became my permanent family. God became my Father, replacing my dad who showed very little love.

Chapter 16

WHERE CAN WE FIND TRUE TRUTH? RELIABLE TRUTH.

S ociety is no help. All we hear coming out of our government is lies and more lies. Politicians are all focused on what is politically correct not what is best for our country. Like many marriages it is a battle of "he said, she said." It is becoming easier for television news and shows to tell fabrications. Today, for the most part, people are not looking for truth. Yet the truth is sitting at their table or hidden in a drawer; God's truth is the Bible. Today the key word is *entitlement*. It's all about entitlement. The pervasive attitude goes like this: "I don't have to work or get a good education if someone else takes care of me. This freedom of do-nothing is great. Let the government take care of me, and if I should decide to go to work I want all the benefits of a good steady paycheck, health insurance, and vacations immediately. I am entitled to this!"

Every young person should have to read *The Greatest Generation* by Tom Brokaw. I am a proud member of that generation. We are fast dying out. I want to shout: "Wake up young America. Take a good look at what your grandparents accomplished so you would have a decent life." The questions our younger folks should ask — What is your attitude about God? Who is God? Is he for real or just a figment of imagination? Time to reconsider the path you are on.

J.B. Philips wrote a book entitled *Your God is Too Small: A Guide for Believers and Skeptics Alike*. He begins the book by showing how in the minds of many people God is not big enough for all that has transpired in the modern world with all the scientific advancements. In our conscience God is inadequate to meet our every day challenges of life. He gives a number of examples how we misjudge God's authority and power. One example talks about how the Bible begins in the Garden of Eden lost and ends with the Garden of Eden (paradise) restored. Philips recounts adult counseling sessions by psychiatrists and illustrates the role conscience plays in a person's life. If, for example a person had strict parents who were overly authoritative and domineering they may view God as a fiery tyrant who reminds them of the way they were treated by their parents. There are so many homes with children without fathers. From my perspective, no matter how hard mothers try to raise their children to become good and responsible citizens they cannot provide the discipline, love and truthful guidance a devoted father and husband can give.

Then there are those who confuse the voice of their conscience as God talking to them. The old adage 'let conscience be your guide' can get one into a whole peck of trouble especially if we have not learned to discern and choose the right over wrong path to take. Phillips points out that it is extremely unlikely we shall ever be moved to worship God or go to church on our own initiative. We have become too narcissistic. Only God's Holy Spirit can wake us up before it is too late. Unless there is a God by whom *right* and *wrong* can be reliably assessed, moral judgments can be no more than opinion. Your opinion is as good as my opinion when it comes to a moral sense and judgment. In order to reach an understanding of who God is we need help outside of ourselves. And this is where the Holy Spirit comes in to do his work by convincing us that God is who he says he is. The truth is that unless one believes and receives the Father's promises by faith he cannot enter the kingdom of heaven. God has created us that we might worship him only. This is God's VOICE speaking in John 16:8-9:

> *"And when the Holy Spirit comes He will convict the world of sin, and of righteousness, and judgment.*
> *Of sin, because they do not believe in Me.*
> *Of righteousness because I go to my Father, and you see me not,*
> *Of judgment because the prince of this world is judged."*

When I was a pastor in California a few people were always coming up to me with their pat answers for not believing the Bible. They thought the Bible was full of myths, not for intelligent people. They criticized it as highly unorganized and full of errors. Their skeptical rationales include—*"If there is a God why does he let man destroy himself (free will)? How can God allow some people to suffer and commit suicide (free will)? If God does really exist he set the world in motion, wound it like a clock and went off to play with other planets in the universe.*

Jesus said there will always be wars and rumors of war until the end. It is important we spend time in the book of Genesis, the beginning, because it is God's VOICE speaking through his chosen instruments. Here we read of the joy he had in bringing the first family into the world. This was his crowning achievement. "And God said, let us make man in our image, according to our likeness, and let them rule...God created man of the dust of the ground and breathed into his nostrils the breath of life, and man became a living soul."—Genesis 1:26-28 This is the plurality of God, by inference, God the Father, God the Son and God the Holy Spirit.

Doubters, agnostics and atheists need to begin with the Supreme Being. Just because one denies God or his existence does not mean God does not exist. In fact, it proves his existence even more so because fools have said there is no God and by man's foolishness he will never know God. God gives these doubters up to believe their own mantra. On judgment day they will stand before God and hear these condemning words: "...depart from me, you who love your sin, for I never knew you."—Mathew 7:23

I studied Genesis to see how God declares his existence and displays his creative power. "And God said (His VOICE), let us make man in our image" –Genesis 1:26 A likeness but not identical, man is like God and is God's representative. The Hebrew words are very clear and need no further clarification. Our likeness as man/woman is like God in a finite way. "In fact as we read the Scriptures, we realize that a full understanding of mans likeness to God would require a full understanding of who God is in His being and His actions and a full understanding of who man is and what he does." Wayne Grudem, *Systematic Theology: An Introduction to Biblical Doctrine*.

Are we physically like God? No. "God is Spirit and they that worship Him must worship Him in spirit and truth."—John 4:24 Are we morally like God, capable of knowing what is good, righteous and truthful? And what is the opposite, evil? Are we mentally like God? Are we rational able to respond in a finite way as God responds in an infinite way? God communicates with man in personal ways using reason and intelligence. In the Garden of Eden God spoke to Adam and Eve as two, intelligent human beings. That open communication has not changed. Isaiah 1:18 says: "Come, let us reason together, though your sins are as scarlet they shall be white as snow."

God does not reason with the animals he directs them and has put man in charge of them. Horses were trained to ride into battle; plow the fields for planting grain, to serve man. We put bits in their mouths to control their movements and harness their energy. Man without God is like a wild horse out of control. When man finally comes under God's control he becomes a different person. Rebellion (self will) and insubordination has clouded our minds and our vision has distorted what we had in the beginning. "Jesus Christ is the image of the invisible God." (II Corinthians 4:4;Col. 1:15) God has predestined us "to be conformed to the image of His Son."—Rom. 8:28-29 One writer calls this 'the everlastingness of God.' God never ends but is forever and ever.

Romans 8:28 says: "And we know that ALL THINGS work together for good to them that love God, to them who are called according to His purpose. For whom he did foreknow, he also did procrastinate to be conformed to his image of his Son, that he might be the firstborn among many brethren." This means that God is sovereign in ALL THINGS. Whether it is by life or death, God is sovereign. Paul said: "...for to me to live is Christ, to die is gain." When we attend a funeral we rightly eulogize the deceased as it provides a catharsis for the bereaved. It allows for a purifying of emotions, the alleviation of fears and anxiety in knowing that we have the peace of God that surpasses all understanding. John 14-17: "My peace I leave with you..." As a pastor I took part in many funerals. The ones that gave me the most joy and satisfaction were those who died as Christians. These were true celebrations. Going home to be with the Lord.

Chapter 17

THE MEANING OF DIVINE ELECTION AND THE PREDESTINED WILL OF GOD

There is the divine election and predestined will of God. Divine election means God knows who will elected, that is who will be saved and who will not. Every person's life is in God's hands. This means God knows all things. He hardened Pharaoh's heart in order to demonstrate his power to him and to the Israelites. This is God's omniscience—he is all knowing therefore he knows the hearts of men and women before they even say a word. His sovereignty reigns supreme. It is for us to humbly bow before his throne and worship him as obedient children. "Suffer the little children and forbid them not, for of such is the kingdom of heaven."—Matthew 19:14

If we are to be saved it will happen. Does God see? Does God hear? Does God speak (His VOICE)? Does God enjoy everything he created? Does man possess these same qualities? Does he listen to what God says? "… And God put Adam to sleep and while he slept He took one of his ribs and fashioned a woman and brought her to the man. And Adam said, she is now bone of my bones, and flesh of my flesh and she shall be called woman. And God blessed them and God said to them, be fruitful and multiply, and fill the earth, subdue it and rule over it…And God saw all that He had made, and behold, it was very good."—Genesis 2:21 This must have been beautiful beyond our imagination.

In Genesis 1:26-28; 2:22-25, God tells Adam and Eve to rule over the Garden, take care of it, keep it beautiful. After the fall it took the Psalms, the poets and gifted astronomers to describe the universe. Who can fully describe the beauty of the rainbow? Who can discern the look in the eyes of two lovers or the beauty of a baby? Who can describe the beauty in the lilies of the field or the mountains overlooking the world? Who can deny these wonders, large and small, are all the manifestation of God in all his glory and splendor? Read some of the great songs and hymns that have been written proclaiming the soul's response to God. Read the Psalms of the Old Testament. Only the fool has said in his heart there is no God. To deny God is to deny your self-existence. (Psalm 139) Do you realize how valuable you are as a part of God's kingdom? Before you were born God knew all about you. Read the 139th Psalm in a quiet time of prayer. Often Biblical scholars encourage us to read the Bible out loud.

Vs.1: "O Lord you have searched me and know me."
2: "You know when I sit down and when I rise up."

7: "Where can I go from your Spirit? Where can I flee from your presence?"
13: " You formed my inward parts; you wove me in my mother's womb."
14: "I will give thanks to you, for I am fearfully and wonderfully made."

For a few years I lived in Colorado. I was able to do some climbing on Pike's Peak and near the top I was able to look out over the vast mountain range. I loved to hear the echo rebound when I yelled "HELLOOOOO." I marveled at the grand and majestic Tetons in Wyoming. I drank in the beauty of Yellowstone with the Old Faithful geyser exploding into the heavens. I smelled the sulfuric mud pots and the scalding beauty of Morning Glory Pool. I have traveled to Mt. Lassen and climbed to the top of the highest peak. For several summers I have driven through the California Gold Rush towns exploring the 49er Trail. I even owned property in the California mountains of Swansboro Gold Rush country. I listened to the giant pines talking to each other in the early morning wind.

I have been up to Big Sky Montana with my niece and our family. As we were getting ready to depart suddenly two glorious rainbows flashed across the mountain peaks. My wife and I have walked along the seashore of California's Carmel Valley with the ocean waves sweeping across the sandy beach drenching our toes. I have filled my senses with the beauty of tulips and various flowers springing up as we drove across America. Who created all this beauty and wonder? Tell me if you dare that there is no Creator God. Gen. 1:1: "…

the heavens declare the glory of God and His firmament displays His glory." Only the fool has said in his heart, there is no God. But wait. There is hope for all who can set aside prejudices, biases and preconceived ideas for a moment. Admit this is a most beautiful story. More importantly, it is true.

Chapter 18

GOD'S GIFT OF FREE WILL

This brings us to God's gift of free will. In the beginning God told Adam and Eve they could eat from every tree in the Garden, "…but of the tree of the knowledge of good and evil you may not eat of it for you will die."—Genesis 2:17. Walter Brueggemann, author of Genesis: *Interpretation: A Bible Commentary for Teaching and Preaching,* and Professor of the Old Testament at Columbia Theological Seminary, Decatur, Georgia reminds us that the two trees are incidental and are not the cause of the wrong doing. "It is God's **command** that is important."

As parents we give our children commands all the time and we expect and require obedience. If a child refuses to obey the command there are often consequences. According to Brueggemann, "…human beings before God are characterized by vocation, permission and prohibition. All three facets are to be held together." In the same way, God's command (His VOICE) is a serious one. Now if you don't believe that Adam and Eve were our first parents then you have a psychological and spiritual problem because God's Word makes it very clear they were brought forth by God's divine will. Out of the first family came all the families of the world. As the old hymn exalts: '*brown and yellow, black and white all are precious in God's sight.*' It is man himself that has brought about all the calamities and the racial prejudice and hatred. God's VOICE says love your neighbor as yourself. It is better to give than receive. Love suffers long and is kind. Love is the greatest gift of all. (I Corinthians 13)

From our first family came blessing, new birth and a curse, the first murder. In the Garden man was immediately given free choice. Free will and free

choice is written in nature and stamped on the soul of every baby born. God provided everything for their happiness and success; even eternal life.

But Adam and Eve decided on their own it was more important to become like God, to become as wise as God. They chose their own autonomy over a personal relationship with their Creator. Thus began the worship of man. Three things happened in the fall; man died spiritually, he no longer had fellowship with God, and he died physically, death passed on the whole human race.

While in the Garden, at first, Adam and Eve didn't have to turn over the soil. Every vegetable and fruit was available for the harvesting. All they had to do was pick it. They lived in a perfect climate and harmony with their Creator. They talked with God freely. Everything they saw in the Garden was beautiful and untainted by sin. They were not conscious of their nakedness. It never entered their head. God made every provision for them and he put them in charge.

Adam was highly intelligent as was Eve, his help-
mate. He named all the plants, animals, birds and sea
life. He was not bent over like an animal but walked
upright, straight and tall. Every child born of Adam and
Eve's seed bears their generic code. All the animals were
born 'after their kind.' There was no crossing over from
an ape to an orangutan as evolutionists would have us
believe. We did not rise up out of the slime and tar pits.
Man retained his dignity and identity as "after God's
likeness, a living breathing human soul."—Genesis 2:7

What happened to change all this beautiful setting?
To start with God's perfect love cast out fear. Adam and
Eve walked and talked with God with no fear. They
knew His VOICE. Like a parent who loves their child,
the child senses that love and has no fear. Like the wife
who loves her husband, and the husband who loves his
wife neither knows fear. She has no trepidation when
he is near because she knows he will protect her. The
first parents had this same relationship with their Father.
When this perfect love was cast aside and fear, doubt and
disappointment emerged. They exchanged the truth and
righteousness of God for a lie. They began to fear his
VOICE. Our earthly father may disappoint us and we
may transfer this failure to our Father in heaven, but God
loves us and sent his Son to prove it.(John 3:16; John 14).

Dr. Walter Bruggemann puts it like this in his commentary on Genesis: "This story is a theological cri-
tique of anxiety. It presents a prism through which the
root cause of anxiety can be understood... The man and
the woman are controlled by their anxiety. (Genesis3:1)
They seek to escape anxiety by hiding from God, because
fear has to do with punishment, and he who fears is not

perfected in love. Fear casts out love and leaves only desire." (Gen. 3:10). He continues: "Anxiety comes from doubting God's providence, from rejecting his care and seeking to secure our own well-being without God."

That's a mouthful but think it through. People are fraught with fear and anxiety; they have no peace as they mature and grow older and attend funerals of friends and family. Each time they ask themselves *'Is that person in heaven? Were they a Christian?'* They know death looms constantly before them. Shakespeare's Hamlet tells of the dread of death. God's perfect love casts out fear. Proverbs 1:7: "The fear of the Lord is the beginning of wisdom. Perfect love casts out fear." Psalm 27:1: "The Lord is my light and salvation; whom shall I fear? The Lord is the strength of my life; whom shall I be afraid?" Philippians 4:6: "Be anxious for nothing, but in everything by prayer and supplication with thanksgiving let your requests be made known to God."

Be anxious for nothing. As we live out our lives we are bombarded daily with making the right decisions. As the decisions pile up we become more stressed—*'Did I do the right thing? What more can I do? What if I make a mistake? Who can I turn to for help?'* Jesus said, "Take my yoke upon you and learn from, for I AM gentle and humble in heart, and you will find rest for your souls, for My yoke is easy and My burden is light."—Matthew 11:29-30 Wow. Permanent rest is found only in Jesus Christ, he alone can lift our burdens. What a passage to live by. Jesus says: "Let not your heart be troubled, believe in God believe also in me."—John 14:1 ff.

Similar to this first beatitude, "Blessed (happy) are the poor in spirit, for theirs is the kingdom of heaven,"— Matthew 5:3 Christian pastor and author John MacArthur points out "The only ones who will hear are those who are burdened by their own spiritual bankruptcy and the weight of trying to save themselves by keeping the law." They have to realize that salvation is not in anything they can do, it is the sovereign work of God on the heart. Jesus Christ, by his Holy Spirit must awaken within the heart and soul of man giving God's love and free gift of new life. Jesus warns us that there is a greater fear we should take action. Matthew 10:28: "Do not fear those who kill the body but are unable to kill the soul, but rather fear Him who is able to destroy both body and soul in hell." Persecution only harms the physical body. God alone controls what happens to the spiritual soul. To ignore God's VOICE pleading to follow his Son is to place your body and soul in jeopardy of eternal judgment and loss.

On this point I wonder how many people just go merrily along in life and forget they have a soul thirsting for God. There is no problem when it comes to the body. We do everything we can to nourish it, feed it and spend millions on keeping it young. Look at all the 'wonder drugs' we consume every year. Look at all the so-called Fountain of Youth cosmetics slathered on to keep the face, hands and body from aging. When I look in the mirror each morning now, I see the chicken tracks on my face getting larger. But one thing I am sure of, Jesus Christ is by my side and I no longer am afraid of tomorrow because I know he holds my hand. The dark reaper creeps up on us slowly, but he is a defeated foe. Do not fear whatever happens to destroy the body, but rather take God's VOICE seriously. He says "…fear Him who is able to destroy both body and soul in hell."— Matthew 10:28 He is referring to the final judgment for rejecting Jesus.

Chapter 19

OVERCOMING TEMPTATION BY REFUSING TO ACCEPT IT

D o not accept temptation! When all hell breaks loose and we don't know what will happen next let the peace of Christ fill your soul. As Jesus was about to make his departure to heaven he told his disciples to remember he is the fountain of peace. "Let not your heart be troubled neither let it be afraid. My peace I give unto you not as the world thinks of their kind of momentary peace, my peace floods the soul and comfort the heart."—John 14.1-3-27

Where did temptation come from? Certainly God does not tempt anyone. Temptation came not from within the Garden but from the outside. There were already fallen angels so sinning did not surprise God. He knew it would come from the voluntary moral choices people make. There was nothing wrong with Adam and Eve morally, physically or mentally. They were perfect in every way. But they were given free will and needed to keep it under control.

Would they worship their creator or the creature? The tempter was a beautiful fallen angel before he crawled in the dust on the ground. The first couple had no idea that evil lurked in the shadows. Temptation came from a fallen angel that was craftier than any beast of the field. It is said that Satin was a fallen archangel with a supernatural spirit that possessed the beautiful slithering body of a snake. What is it about snakes that frighten and repel us? We sense their danger and we flee.

Isa. 14:11-14: "...how art thou fallen from Heaven, O Lucifer, son of the morning? How art thou cut down to the ground, which didst weaken the nations? " Because he said in his heart, "I will ascend into the heavens, I will exalt my throne above the stars of God." and later, "Yet you shall be brought down to hell, to the sides of the pit." Satan uses his authority to challenge God's authority. (I John 3:8) What better person to test his power on than Eve, the mother of all living. Why did he turn to Eve? Why not Adam? Was she more easily influenced because she possessed a mother's heart? Eve was the representative of all women. Should she have called Adam and discussed it with him? Why didn't she ask God? You decide. Satin found her alone. The test was to keep God's command and trust in God's care. Once ambition and pride set in there is a short cut...God's command can be circumvented.

Women who ignore the message of the Bible regarding the role they should play in God's plan for marriage find themselves relying on their '*I-want-a-bees*.' And men are not any better off in this regard. Could it be that God's restrictions are too harsh? Satan called Eve's attention to God's command: "Has God said you shall not touch it or eat it, lest you die? You shall not die, God knows that if you do you will become like God, knowing good and evil." (Satan knows the Bible and tested Jesus with it. The English Standard Version Bible commentary puts it like this: *Adam and Eve's rebellion against God is an ongoing damaging conflict between husband and wife within marriage, driven by the sinful behavior of both in rebellion against their respective God-given roles and responsibilities in marriage.* I recommend reading Emerson Eggerich's *Love and Respect* as it is written to help both husband and wife.

The true pattern for marriage founded on the redemptive work of Christ is set out in Ephesians 5:21-32. There are many reasons why marriages fail.

Look at the three temptations of Christ and how he responded. (Matthew 4:1-10) Here the Christian is given plenty of ammunition to defeat the devil's hammer. Ask what do you see about Christ's temptations that could be applied to the success of a marriage?

First, Satan tested Christ's authority challenging— "If you are the Son of God?" Does this sound familiar? Doubters are still asking this same question today. They are the philosophers, atheists, agnostics, scientists, and Darwinist. Jesus quoted scripture back to Satan: "It is written, man shall not live by bread alone, BUT BY EVERY WORD THAT PROCEEDS OUT OF THE MOUTH OF GOD." (His VOICE)—Matthew 4:4 When reading the Bible be in a quiet place to allow for true meditation. Listen for the Spirit to speak to you. While reading the Bible there are certain verses that stand out, grabbing our attention. Meditate on these verses that speak directly to you. Take advantage of these meditative moments to ask the Holy Spirit to help you. He will.

Second, the devil took Jesus to the holy city and made him stand on the sacred pinnacle of the Temple and again asked this question: "If you are the Son of God throw yourself down and the angels will save you." Jesus answer: "You shall not put the Lord your God to the test."—Matthew 4:7; Deuteronomy 6:16 Have we denied the Lord in our marriage decisions?

Third, the devil took Jesus to a high mountain showing him all the kingdoms of the world, and all their glory. The devil said, "…all these things will I give You, IF YOU BOW DOWN AND WORSHIP ME."—Matthew 4:9 Here Satan reveals he actually believed he had more power and authority than Jesus. In our fallen humanity man actually thinks he has this same ability to fulfill God's righteous demands by his own good works.

Jesus answered Satan: "…be-gone…for it is written, YOU SHALL WORSHIP THE LORD YOUR GOD, AND SERVE HIM ONLY."—Matthew 4:10 Then the devil left. Time and time again Jesus quoted 'it is written' referring back to God's Word. Satan was and is today a defeated foe when our lives are in the care of Jesus Christ. We have nothing to fear for he has guaranteed our safety and peace of mind. Jesus said: (His VOICE) "My peace I leave with you; my peace I give to you. Let not your heart be troubled neither let it be afraid."—John 14:27. Perfect peace casts out fear. Going back to verse one: "Let not your hearts be troubled. Believe in God; believe also in me." If you have locked out the Lord in marriage he is outside knocking on our door?

Chapter 20

To Believe is an Imperative

This next section is full of Christ's VOICE speaking to us: The word BELIEVE is considered an imperative. Not only believe, keep on believing, never stop believing. Jesus is the life giver, the one who, once you place your faith, trust and hope brings peace to the heart and soul. In the world you will have tribulation; there is no peace. That which was lost regardless of the world's rejection of the truth, Jesus Christ brings peace and rest to the soul.

Without full commitment to trust in God no one can have any peace in this world. That's why his coming is so important. "In the world you will have tribulation, but be of good cheer for I have overcome the world."—John 16:33 From Matthew 11:29: "Come unto ME, all who are heavy laden, and I will give you rest. Take my yoke upon you and learn from Me, for I AM gentle and humble in heart, and you will find rest for your souls." Lean not on your own understanding (knowledge, reason), but in all your ways acknowledge him and he will direct the path you take. A person will never realize just how much peace they have in mind, body and spirit until they fully commit to his leading. Here is true rest for your soul. We are a lot like C.S. Lewis who came kicking and screaming into the Kingdom. When the VOICE of the Holy Spirit speaks to you it is your time to say '*yes I believe.*'

Proverbs 5:12,13: "How have I hated instruction, and my heart spurned reproof? I have not listened to the VOICE of my teachers, nor inclined my ear to my instructors." In Isaiah 28:23: "Give ear and hear my VOICE, listen and hear my words." Money can't buy it, good works can't guarantee it, but faith can. "Peace in Hebrew is the word, 'SHALOM' which expresses much more than the English word. It conveys the absence of conflict and turmoil and the positive blessing that comes with a right relationship with God."—ESV Study Bible (John 15:18-19; 16:33). In a good marriage there is peace, forgiveness, compassion and compromise. Love never fails. Jesus said: "My Peace I leave with you."—John 14:1ff. Jesus said this to his disciples and all who would listen. Why? They soon would be facing life without him. They would be on their own. Are you all alone? The disciples were just like us, they needed assurance and comfort and love. Jesus gave them all three.

Assurance: "I AM the way the truth and the life…"
Comfort: "I will come again for you, but in the meantime I will send the Holy Spirit to be at your side.
Love: "Lo, I AM with you always, even to the end of ages."

There has never been another living person on earth who could make those statements and keep them.

Take a few moments to think about Jesus' words, his peace now and eternal life in the future. Only the unbelieving have no peace. This is not pie-in-the- sky-by-and-by. In II Timothy 1:7-8 Paul reminds us: "…for God has not given us a spirit of fear, but of power and of love and of a sound mind." Perfect love casts out fear. Paul's life as a Christian was tested again and again. He was stoned. He was left for dead. He was in prison when he wrote the Epistles.

Dear friend, have you turned your life over to him yet? Do it right now.

Why do I keep going back to Genesis and the Garden of Eden? Because this is where the true story began. This is where it all unfolded and people are too prone to forget this truth. Look at the temptations of Adam and Eve. Eve saw the tree was good for food, a delight to the eyes and desirable to make one wise. She ate the fruit and gave it to her husband and he ate. I would like to say right here, after being married for thirty-eight years, I would have obeyed my wife too. We two are one flesh. Picking from the tree is not the important point. They disobeyed the commandment of God. The consequences of breaking God's laws and commandments are many. Fear struck their hearts. They ran away from God to hide from his presence. They were no longer safe and secure.

That day they died spiritually and later would die physically. The Tree of Life was banned forever. Death passed to the whole human race and the ground was also cursed so that it would no longer yield its crops without hard labor. God is not the author of temptation in man for God cannot be tempted. Every man is tempted because of his own greed, dissatisfaction in life or lust. The scripture says each person is tempted when he is carried away by his own desires, when the desire is conceived it gives birth to sin, and when sin is fulfilled it brings forth death. (James 1:3-15)

Their dependence on God vanished. Adam and Eve now had to depend on their own tainted intuition. They relied on their own intellect and powers of reasoning. When God came looking for them they were fearful at what God would do to them. They were naked and ashamed and tried to cover up their bodies with leaves. How often have we tried to cover up our mistakes to keep people from finding out what we have done? We try to bury our secret sins. We have the same old human nature our first parents experienced when they walked out on God. The fall is universal. It is a historical event. It happened in real time. All the players were VERY real. The Bible confirms this in both Testaments. Job 1:20-22: "Job arose, and rent his mantle, and shaved his head, and fell down upon the ground, and worshiped. And said, Naked came I out of my mother's womb, and naked shall I return thither; the Lord gave and the Lord hath taken away, blessed be the name of the Lord,"

The Welsh Protestant, Dr. Lloyd Jones, points out that animals cannot sin. They are not conscious of their bodies. They were not created in the image of God. They have no guilt of sin. When Adam and Eve fell they were condemned within themselves. They knew immediately something happened; fellowship with God was no longer possible. They no longer had a clear relationship with nature. From that moment there was pain in childbearing. The soil would no longer obey their wishes. The ground would be thorny and unyielding. We would need to fight our way through life. Adam and Eve were driven from the Garden and flaming swords were placed at the entrance and exit so they could never return.

Adam would return to the dust of the ground from whence he came. It seems over the centuries man's moral and intellectual powers have declined. From Adam we are all born in sin. Psalms 51:5: "There are those who believe in the guilt part but not the pollution part." Eve began to listen to the slanders against God. "Sin came into the world through one man and death as the result of sin, so death spread to all men…sin was in the world before the Law was given… death held sway from Adam to Moses, the Lawgiver…" The righteousness of Christ has set us free. It is imputed to our account when we believe. Romans 5:19: "For as through one man's disobedience the many were made sinners, even so through the obedience of the One the many will be made righteous."

Evil had to be confronted and defeated if man was ever to return to God's favor. God did not leave them out in the cold. He determined to pronounce judgment on the curse they brought on with their disobedience and restore their lost estate. Genesis 3:15: "The woman's seed will crush that old serpent, the devil and a Deliverer will be born— Jesus Christ the Lord." This was the first sign of the covenant promise from God. It will show up all through the Old Testament. From Noah and the rainbow to father Abraham on into the New Testament with the birth of Jesus Christ.

Therefore, we have a legal declaration by God: justification is a forensic act on the part of God whereby he declares all who believe are saved through the shed blood of Jesus Christ our Lord. His righteousness is imputed to their account and all sins are forgiven and washed away. It is just as though we had never sinned. What was the purpose of the Law? Without the law I would not know I am a sinner. Jesus Christ came and fulfilled the laws demanding the soul that sinned shall die. Death no longer holds its sting. Romans 10:9,10 and 3:19-26 reveals a powerful promise to those who believe. Listen carefully to these words from the Bible:

"If you acknowledge and confess with your lips that Jesus is Lord and in your heart believe that God raised Him from the dead, you will be saved. For with the heart a person believes (relies now on Christ) he is declared righteous, which God accepts, and with the mouth confesses (openly (to others) declaring his faith, confirms he is saved." — Romans 10:9-10

My wife and I have been living in Minnesota going on five years. I am retired and have time to slow down and smell the flowers, enjoy the beautiful landscape of trees and many lakes. People all around us are so busy getting up every morning, having their coffee and rushing off to work. In my morning drive to the gym to get in my daily three mile walk and workout I am continually amazed at how many times I see people drive through stop signs and red lights. They seldom come to a complete stop. Why? They think no one is watching at that early hour.

Last year in March we took a trip to California to see our family friends Don and Kay Bennett. We have been doing this every year since settling in Buffalo, MN. We were tired of the piles and piles of snow and the cold, cold wind chill. So we made our annual trek to Southern Cal. The first thing we noticed in California were all the beautiful flowers in bloom. We hadn't seen flowers growing in several months in Buffalo, MN. What a joy! I took time to get several shots of flowers with my camera. The weather was also very agreeable, in the upper 70s and 80s. So warm and beautiful we felt like we had arrived in paradise; died and gone to heaven. Ha.

The first stops in sunny California included visiting our son and his wife in Los Angeles. Next we spent time with Don and Kay Bennett, our long time friends and god-parents to our children, Curtis and Joy. We spent many Thanksgivings and Christmases together over the years when we still lived in San Bruno, California. After a week with the Bennetts we headed for the Bay Area and San Bruno. Over the years Sharon and I made many wonderful friends. A few years back we would meet for coffee and conversation at Starbucks Coffee shop in Bay Hill Shopping Center. Our coffee group eventually grew to 10 people. We have stayed in contact with these great folks since retiring in 2006 and moving to the Midwest. On this vacation we spent time with this fun group. While in San Bruno we also saw the giant hole a gas pipe made when it exploded and leveled homes just a few weeks earlier. What a real tragedy and loss of life.

The weather did not cooperate with our plans to travel the northern route back to Minnesota so we headed south again and luckily got to spend another two days with the Bennett's. Thank the Lord for friends who care!

Chapter 21

MAN BELIEVES IN HIS EXCUSES MORE THAN GOD'S PROMISES

Why is it so easy for people to disobey the laws meant to protect them? In driving across six states and back the thing that impressed and disturbed me the most was the way people constantly disobeyed the speed limit. If the sign said 60 they went 70, if it said 70 they went 85, if it said 75 they went 85 or 90. It was difficult to stay at the required speed limit without being run over. What is all the rush? I mention this as an example of just one area of man's proclivity towards sin and a rebellious heart. It seems he can't help himself. I wonder what God is thinking? Man knows the laws but he loves to break them. Man avoids knowing God personally because he is spiritually dead. Spiritual things are spiritually discerned and without the Spirit of God (inside you) you cannot understand God's truths. Therefore—MAN BELIEVES IN HIS EXCUSES MORE THAN GOD'S PROMISES.

Man lets his own voice and conscience determine his life. He has no time to find out if God is there. He is encased in a BOX with no windows or doors. He relies on his humanistic philosophy, and we all have one. He is master of his fate. He believes he can solve the moral issues of life by ignoring their existence. In some cases it takes pain to open eyes.

One of the biggest excuses man gives is that everyone interprets the Bible according to their own whim and fancy. No two people agree on what it says. That's why we have so many denominations. This is the devil's lie and he is still the deceiver. We know intuitively that our excuses are there so we don't have to face the fact that God wants to speak (His VOICE) to us personally through the Bible. I dare you to pick up a Bible and read it yourself. Don't rely on anything else, just the Bible. Begin with the gospel of John in the New Testament. Let the WORD speak its message. It is written for you. Quietly ask God to speak his VOICE to you. The Bible has many mysteries that we cannot answer with clarity and certainty. We are finite and God is infinite, but as we give ourselves to the serious study of the Bible many of our questions are answered. I would wager that some of you reading this book this minute don't realize God knows your name, when and where you were born. You don't believe it? Good, now turn to Psalm 139 and read it.

Autonomous man believes in his ability to please God by his benevolent acts. He believes that if he works hard enough in doing unto others God can't turn him down. It would be great if this were true. Dr. Frances Schaeffer, Evangelical Christian theologian, philosopher and Presbyterian pastor, points out that whenever man begins with himself as a starting hypothesis and then proceeds to solve his problems of guilt, disbelief, what's morally right or wrong, cause and effect, he comes to a dead end street. (his Trilogy)

Recently Steve Jobs passed away. While living he accomplished outstanding feats. We are the recipients of his marvelous computer age inventions. At his death it is said over forty thousand people worked for him. What did he find out about life after death? Did his works give him a free pass to heaven? Not according to the Bible. The question is always '*What did you do with Jesus Christ?*'

Many of the great philosophers like Aristotle, Socrates and Plato tried to answer the universal questions about the meaning of life and what is truth. They invariably ended up in despair and some even committed suicide. For some, life ends up being meaningless (this is the theme of the book of Ecclesiastes) and frightful because everything that is tried ends up in despair.

Look at the Hollywood crowd. Study them carefully. They are lost in themselves, their money and sexual promiscuity. When divorces and different partners fail them they often turn to drugs and alcohol. Where are those who made headlines of yesterday? Many ended up as lonely suicides. But we enjoyed their movies and celebrity antics for a time. They are not to be glorified or promoted. They are fictitious, full of perfidy. However, our youth look to them for their dreams and heroes. Our own son dreamed of becoming an actor. He was in plays in high school, attended the Academy of Dramatic Arts and tenaciously tried to break into acting for a career. He finally gave up. We believed in his goal and supported him all the way. And were proud when he earned his SAG card. Today he is very happy in a different occupation.

Jesus said that in the last days there will be those who will say, "Look at what I have done in your name," and he will say, "… depart from me you who take pleasure in iniquity, for I never knew you."—Matthew 7: 21-23; Psalm 6:8. The commandments remind us that we should be doing benevolent acts for others in need. We should deny ourselves when our brother needs a helping hand. We should apply the Golden Rule; do unto others as we would like done to ourselves. But even with all our good deeds, when we have done all we can do, we are only doing what God has told us to do in the first place. It does not mean that we have special privileges or merit with God. Man forgets the first great commandment, "you shall love the Lord your God with ALL your heart, with ALL your soul, and with ALL your mind." The second is like it, you shall love your neighbor as yourself." (Matthew 22:37-39) Also the Sermon of The Hill gives excellent insight into the commandment. (Matthew 5)

Note the word all. When it comes to the inspiration of the Scriptures we find the word ALL. "ALL Scripture is inspired by God…"—II Timothy 3:16,17. Look up the word 'all' in Webster's Dictionary. A whole section is devoted to this word. 'All' says everything, the whole part, all-consuming, and the greatest possible amount. We are to start with God's Word first and last. Some translations change the word 'all.'

When theologian Dietrich Bonhoeffer visited the American Union Seminary in the early thirties he was appalled at what little attention they gave to the Gospel message of salvation. He visited a Negro church located a few blocks away and found the true witness to Jesus Christ. He never forgot this experience and when he returned to Germany he noted that the theological atmosphere at Union was accelerating the process of the secularization of Christianity in America. Don't be deceived. God is not mocked for his Word will accomplish what it is supposed to accomplish regardless of how man denies the truth. Bonhoeffer makes it clear in his writings that a true Christian does not cower or hide his faith behind church walls. Instead he places himself out there in the real world ready to suffer and die if necessary for the cross of Christ. Read his *Cost of Discipleship*. Bonhoeffer took a stand against Nazi Germany's socialistic tyranny and the Reich Church. He paid with death and martyrdom. Read C.S. Lewis' *Mere Christianity*. He was an atheist turned Christian. Today people often laugh at someone who takes their faith seriously. But, the bottom line is faith is no laughing matter. To ridicule the faithful Christian is to play or gamble with your soul. The person who neglects his soul will die without God but still face the judgment.

Chapter 22

THE DIFFERENT KIND OF RIGHTEOUSNESS

The Word of God—his VOICE—is active, alive, powerful… sharper than any two-edged sword. Hebrews 4:12: "God the Father, God the Son and God the Holy Spirit are always at work." If God intends that you will be saved, you will by his power. In the sixteenth century theologian Martin Luther wrestled with this problem of man vs. God's righteousness. In *Martin Luther's Basic Theological Writings* by Timothy F. Lull, we read the discussion based on the Epistle of Paul to the Galatians Church. Lull points out a great difference between Christian righteousness and all the other kinds of man's righteousness.

'*Can man's righteousness really exceed the righteousness of God'?* In *Luther's Theology* Lull outlines the many different kinds of righteousness. I will highlight what I think is most important for our discussion. As yourself which righteousness do you believe in?

1. There is a political righteousness involving princess, legislators lawyers, politicians and philosophers.
2. There is the ceremonial righteousness involving human traditions, sacrifices, rituals, dogmas and the church. Parents may teach righteousness to their children including moral discipline. These may not have anything to do with placating God. We do good and try to be good because we should naturally, but we are not always successful.
3. There is the Righteousness of the Law, the Decalogue which Moses taught. There is the Torah.
4. Over and above all these there is the Righteousness of Faith or Christian Righteousness. There is a great distinction betweenthis and all the other definitions for they are contrary to this. They all consist of our good works.
5. There is Active Righteousness involving what man can do on his own.
6. There is a Passive Righteousness which is the Christian Righteousness by faith through Jesus Christ. This is without works. It is hidden in a mystery and the non-Christian world cannot understand it. Christians many times cannot understand it themselves. It is the FREE gift of God imparted to the soul that believes. Human reason cannot resist Active Righteousness which is its own righteousness. It cannot understand Passive Righteousness because it is a work of God that is imparted to his children by the Holy Spirit. It is the Righteousness of Grace, Mercy and the Forgiveness of Sins.

7. Luther points out that both are necessary but must be kept within their limits. Active Righteousness applies to the old law and the old person who is born of flesh and blood. Passive Righteousness means WE DO NOTHING, WE HEAR NOTHING ABOUT WORKS, but receive the finished work Christ did for us on the cross. It is two little words—"FOR US"on the cross. Sin no longer reigns in our bodies and controls our lives. It doesn't mean we no longer get ourselves into trouble, but now we ask for forgiveness and proceed to quit doing it with God's help and cleansing. When a person receives Jesus Christ the Holy Spirit becomes their strong advocate, comforter and guide. By faith we follow Christ and our bodies are now the temple of the Holy Spirit and we are God's possession. The Holy Spirit confirms this: "If you walk in the Spirit you no longer desire to obey the lusts of the flesh."— Romans, 8th chapter.

Salvation is an individual thing. President Obama was asked the question regarding his faith and he said, "I believe in collective righteousness." He obviously does not know the Bible. It is not 'collective righteousness' where I can be saved for you and others, that idea is found nowhere in the Bible. From Luther we learn, man is more concerned about Active Righteousness (what he can do), the Golden Rule, than Passive Righteousness (here you do nothing but accept God's promises FOR US). Read Ephesians 1:4: "Even as (in his Love) He chose US." "God actually picked US out for himself as his own- predestined in Christ before the foundation of the world, that we should be holy (consecrated and set apart for him) and blameless in His sight, even above reproach, before Him in love."—Amplified New Testament

Chapter 23

HIS VOICE: THE OLD TESTAMENT SPEAKS AGAIN

I n the Old Testament we discover God spoke (his VOICE) his Word to many of the Old Testament prophets such as Moses, Joshua, Nehemiah, Job, Isaiah, Jeremiah, Ezekiel, Daniel and the Minor Prophets. Let's consider a few of these.

In the Old Testament God gave the Israelites his Words and his laws, the Ten Commandments, for them to live by. He gave them his covenant promise beginning with Noah and the rainbow in the sky. Then through Abraham's seed.

All through their wanderings and wilderness experiences God's presence was with them as is evidenced in his speaking through his prophets and chosen vassals. They had his constant reminder; his VOICE, "I AM that I AM will be with you." God chose this kingdom, this nation to be his instrument to give his Word to the world. (Exodus 20:1-26; Deut. 4:13, 24; Isa. 43:21). When you open the Bible and begin with the book of Genesis you read that it begins with "In the beginning GOD....". They never questioned God's existence. They were his witnesses proclaiming that there is only one God. They practiced monotheism and went out to warn the surrounding nations, who worshiped many false gods, images and idols.

Whenever the Israelites became impatient and disobedient to God he had to speak to them face to face. They were not to go whoring after other gods and idol worship. In his anger he punished their rebellion by allowing their capture by the Meads, the Persians, the Assyrians and the Babylonians. These captivities spanned many decades. When Moses wrote the Pentateuch (the Septuagint), first five books of Bible, there was only one God, the Lord God Almighty (El Shadai).

Even a cursory reading of the life of the Israelites shows us the results of their continued disobedience, repentance and recovery by God's grace. God never gives them up but all through their history we see how again and again they are brought low. God will use them to fulfill his eternal plan of redemption and forgiveness through his only begotten Son, Jesus Christ. It is because of Jesus Christ that God never gives up on us.

NOAH

With the cleansing flood of the earth God speaks to Noah and his family. Genesis 6:8: "... and Noah found favor in the eyes of God." Noah had three sons, Shem, Ham and Japheth. By this time the earth had become corrupt and was filled with violence. Then God said— his VOICE— to Noah, "The end of all flesh has come before me...I am about to destroy them,,, Make yourself an ark... and I am bringing the flood of water upon the earth... I will establish My covenant with you... and lastly, Noah did according to all that God commanded him."—Genesis 6: 13-22.

For forty days and forty nights the flood came upon the earth and all flesh perished except Noah and his family. At the end of the rain Noah and his family came out of the Ark. The first thing they did was worship God. God fulfilled his covenant with Noah and set his bow (a rainbow) in the sky. (6:12-15). Why is it that God punished the wicked? Very often we hear of the righteous suffering with the wicked. Why is that? God is no respecter of persons. Every time you see a rainbow are you reminded of God?

In order to understand the decisions God makes about life and death, who will live and who will die, you have to acknowledge the complete and absolute sovereignty of God in all things. He is the All Mighty, the all knowing (omniscience), powerful God. It is difficult to comprehend this because of our fallen nature. We are finite where God in infinite. We can't think of anything as being absolute, because we design our own rules to suit each of our life's situations. If it feels good to do it as long as you are not hurting anyone else.

ABRAHAM

Here is a beautiful story as true to life today as it was during Abraham and Sari's life. Take time to read this story in Genesis 15-23. This is better than any novel you will ever read. God has his encounter with Abraham. He speaks to Abraham personally. Abraham and Sari are elderly and still they have not given birth to an heir. Yet,

God promised them an heir. The Word of the Lord came to Abraham saying out of your body shall come an heir. And your descendants shall be as the stars in heaven. Abraham believed the Lord and it was reckoned (put to his account) as righteousness.

Did God keep His promised to Abraham? As they were both up in age and even though God promised them a child, they both doubted. Finally, in desperation and disobedience, Sarai told her husband to sleep with the Egyptian maid Hagar and have an heir by her. So eighty-six year old Abraham slept with Hagar and she conceived. Ishmael was born. Hebrew women prided themselves in providing an heir. In some instances it was a disgrace to be barren. With the joy of a new son and the sorrow of being barren Sari becomes very jealous and angry. Hagar becomes so frightened she flees for her life. This is a perfect example of what can happen when we do not listen to God.

The angel of the Lord intercedes for Hagar. (Here is a good example how God uses his angels as ministering spirits.) She is to return to her mistress and submit herself to her authority. The angel reminds Hagar she will have many descendants.

There are always consequences that follow when we doubt God and act on our own stubborn will. God has already spoken to Abraham and made a covenant promise to him. His VOICE to Abraham: "I AM the Lord who brought you out of Ur of the Chaldeans, to give you this land to possess it."— Gen. 15: 3-7 In Genesis chapter 17, Abraham is ninety-nine years old and still no heir. The Lord appeared again and said (his VOICE) to Abraham: "I AM God Almighty; walk before Me and be blameless, and I will establish My covenant between Me and you… And Abraham fell on his face, and God talked to him. You will be the father of multitudes and your name is changed to Abraham. His seed will increase and multiply as the sand on the sea." When we personally are confronted with God speaking directly to us what else can we do but fall on our face before him and worship him. "The Lord seeks those who will worship Him in spirit and in truth."—John 4:24 Do you realize what this means? It assures that we now have a direct channel to the Father through the Son and the Holy Spirit because of the cross and Jesus Christ. God no longer sees our sins because he sees his Son and we are forgiven and justified as though we had never sinned. Jesus paid for us all. Wow.

Later God changes Sarai's name to Sarah (Vs,15) and tells her, "…and she will bear you a son and you will call his name Isaac." Sarah laughed at God. She thought she was too old to bear a child. And God said, "Is anything too difficult for the Lord?" The rest of the story is history and worthy of reading. I want you to get the feeling that God speaks to us when we least expect it. God is there all the time. "Be still and know that I AM God."—II Chronicles 7:14.

In the New Testament book of Hebrews the eleventh chapter, we read all about 'The Triumph of Abraham's faith.' "By faith Abraham, when he was called, obeyed by going out to a place which he was to receive an inheritance; and he went out, not knowing where he was going. For he was looking for the city which has foundation, whose architect and builder is God." Abraham's faith was based wholly on the righteousness of God.

"ABRAHAM BELIEVED GOD, AND IT WAS COUNTED TO HIM AS RIGHTEOUSNESS."— Romans 4:3

This is what is important to think about in this story:
1. We are still in the Old Testament story of Abraham
2. Jesus Christ had not come upon the scene as yet
3. So, where was Abraham's faith?
4. It rested on the promises of God, who is faithful
5. Therefore, this righteousness was imputed to Abraham's account, and to all those who believed by faith.

MOSES

In the Old Testament God Speaks (his VOICE) personally to Moses. Here is one of the most beautiful and powerful conversations between Moses and God. Why is this important? Because people outside the Bible have trouble with the idea of a personal God who knows us so very well and understands us, our needs and speaks to them. Read Exodus, 3rd Chapter for enjoyment. Moses is minding his business out in the fields tending the sheep of Jethro, his father-in-law, priest of Median, on the west side of the mountain of God. Moses has two of his shepherd dogs with him well trained in handling sheep. Suddenly the silence is broken when Moses hears a crackling sound. He turns and sees on the mountainside there is a bush burning but is not consumed. His curiosity compels him to go investigate. As he got near he hears a voice. God was waiting for him. Notice: it was not until Moses turned aside to examine the bush that he found out God was waiting for him. Perhaps it is not until we are willing to stop all our busyness and be still that we will find the Lord waiting for us. (his VOICE) "Be still, and know that I AM God."—Psalm 46:10

We witness the suffering in bondage in Egypt. It is time to send Moses to free the Israelites. At first Moses who was nurtured and educated as part of the Pharoah's court, refuses to go as he remembers his past cruelty experienced at the command of the Pharaoh. To go back meant certain death. This story is worth repeating....God speaks to Moses again (his VOICE), "I will certainly be with you." Moses, still frightened asks God, "...who shall I tell them has sent me?" God replies, "Tell them the God of your fathers, Abraham, Isaac and Jacob has sent me to you." Moses replies, "What if they say to me ' what is His name?' And God replies, "Tell them I AM that I AM has sent you, this is my name forever." Moses asks for Aaron, the priest, to go with him and God agrees. It is certain that the Holy Spirit went before Moses and guided him all the way.

Exodus 33:11 is another great example of God communicating with Moses directly (his VOICE). As Dr. Lloyd Jones points out in his analysis this is a most important passage considering the doctrine of revelation. God told Moses that he was going to accede (give into) Moses request, that he would manifest his glory to him. Moses uttered that great desire: "Show me thy glory..." Moses was worried that was giving him a great task of leading the Israelites. He wanted to know who would help him in this task. "Before I can do this great work," said Moses, "I want to know that your presence will accompany me." God said, "My presence shall go with thee."

When Moses became bold and declared: "show me thy glory," Then God told Moses (his Voice) that it is impossible to see God face to face. "...for no man can see Me in that sense and live. Nevertheless I will reveal my glory to you. So God took Moses and placed him in the cleft of the rock, and then He covered him with His hand."—Exodus 33 God the eternal Spirit, condescended to speak of himself in human terms, and to act in a human manner. He covered Moses with his hand and then he passed by and Moses was only allowed to see his shadowy form, but Moses saw God.

This is a staggering statement. God gave a glimpse of himself to a human being so that men and women might know something about him. Moses persisted in his determination to know God better. He was not disappointed. What about those of us who have never seen God or Jesus Christ? In the Old Testament God made his covenant promise to father Abraham: "Out of thy seed shall all the nations be blessed."—Genesis 22:18 How were these people saved? Jesus Christ was only the message of the prophets concerning the coming Messiah. They believed by faith and the righteousness of Christ was imputed to their account.

God spoke to Moses "FACE TO FACE," Exodus 33:11 says he spoke to him as a man who understood the power and authority of God, as a man speaks to his friend. In Vs. 27 the Lord speaks (his VOICE) to Moses: "...write these Words from the Ten Commandments." Does this sound like a God who is uncaring, out there somewhere in the universe? Stop and think about this encounter that God had with Moses. Can God speak to us today? Is he a personal God who hears and understands our pain, our sorrows? Isn't this what Jesus Christ is talking about when he said, "I will not leave you comfortless, but will send the Holy Spirit?"—John 14-18 Have we experienced the Holy Spirit in our lives lately? Do we even know he exists? Read John, chapters 14-17.

When we come to the book of Numbers we find the words, "...and God speaks (his VOICE) to Moses..." over and over again as he was leading the people of Israel. And Moses did what the Lord told him to do. What is important here is that it is God's voice speaking to his trusted servant. People today just can't believe that God is ready to talk to them right where they stand. God is ever present with us.

JOSHUA

The name 'Joshua' means 'Jehovah saves' and corresponds to the New Testament name for Jesus. Later in the story Moses he turns his leadership over to Joshua. Joshua is son of Nun, the Ephriamite. Joshua is servant under Moses. Joshua was born into Egyptian slavery, trained under Moses and was God's choice to lead Israel into Canaan. He was nearly ninety years old when he became Israel's leader. He died at age 110. John MacArthur writes that Moses talks to God and asks him to appoint his successor.(Numbers 27:15- 23) So the Lord speaks (his VOICE) to Moses: "Take Joshua the son of Nun, a man in whom is the Spirit, and lay your hand on him." And Moses did just as the Lord said. Here is an instance of the laying the hand, a symbol of anointing, the Holy Spirit at work. (Deuteronomy 34:9)

ISAIAH

This is one of the great prophetic books of the Old Testament. Isaiah receives his vision from the Lord and is touched with fire (a symbol of cleansing and purity) (Isaiah 6:1-6). In Isaiah verse 8 he receives his orders from God to address the nation of Israel. In Isaiah 7:14 we read, "Therefore the Lord Himself will give you a sign (God' VOICE), Behold, a virgin will be with child and bear a son, and she will call His name Emmanuel." And in Isaiah 9:6: "For a child will be born to us, a son will be given to us and the government will rest upon His shoulders; and His name shall be caked Wonderful, Counselor, Mighty God, Eternal Father, the Prince of Peace." This is a direct Messianic reference to Jesus Christ to be born of the Virgin Mary, and He will bring forgiveness and peace to all those who will put their faith and trust in Him." Isaiah makes it clear who this person will be, a savior, Jesus Christ the Lord.

God's VOICE speaks to the prophet Isaiah. This is one of the great Messianic books of the Old Testament and worthy of your attention. Here is a great poem, a song of deliverance and celebration. For out of bondage and despair there is rejoicing and freedom. Don't take my word for it, read it for yourself and you will be blessed. One great statement is: "Come, let us reason together, says the Lord. Though your sins are as scarlet, they will be as white as snow; though they are red like crimson, they will be like wool," — Isaiah 1:18

Continuing in Isaiah 1:18: "God has had enough of man's hollow reasoning. Stop your reasoning and turn to the one true God and worship Him. Isaiah heard the VOICE of the Lord, saying: "Whom shall I send, and who will go for us?" Then I said, "Here am I send me." And God said, "Go and tell the people." (Isaiah 6:8). Isaiah spent his whole life doing God's will. King Ahaz was asked to call for a sign but he refused because he feared the Lord. This is worth repeating: "Therefore the Lord Himself will give you a sign; Behold, a virgin shall be with child and bear a son, and she will call His name Emmanuel." (Meaning God is with us.) In Isaiah 7:10-16; Isaiah 53 tells us of the suffering Servant. This section includes early prophecies of the coming of Christ. Read the entire section to understand the coming of the Messiah.

This is Messianic (speaking of the future). In the New Testament book of Luke 1:26-31: "God sent the angel Gabriel to Mary, the virgin and said, "Behold, you will conceive in your womb, and bear a son, and you shall name Him Jesus." He will be great and He will be called the Son of the Most High." Isaiah prophesied the birth of Jesus 700 years before the birth of Christ. Before we are ready to discard this witness as foolishness we need to consider carefully how it affects our eternal destiny.

JEREMIAH

The prophet speaks and God's VOICE speaks. "Now the word of the Lord came to me saying, "Before I formed you in the womb I knew you, and before you were born I consecrated you. I have appointed you a prophet to the nations."—Jeremiah 1:5 This is the omniscient God telling Jeremiah he had plans for him before he was born, God had his destiny all planned out. This is where God chooses certain people to do his bidding and anoints them before they are born. This happened to John the Baptist and with the birth of Jesus Christ. At first

Jeremiah resisted God because of his youth. This passage reminds one of Psalm 139:13, where the psalmist declares the all knowing creative power of God: "You formed my inward parts, you wove me in my mother's womb. I will give thanks to Thee, for I am fearfully and wonderfully made." This passage declares that we all are in God's hands and we all are of great value and worth to him. What we have to do is acknowledge God loves us so much that he willingly sent down his only begotten Son to die for us and we are to believe in him by faith and enter into the second birth.

Jeremiah is worried about being young: "I am a youth no one will listen to me." He was very young like David, the shepherd boy. (19-21yrs old) He didn't know what to say, he was astonished. He was not a brash kid. He was the son of Hilkiah, a priest, so he was well aware of his service to God. The son of a priest is dedicated to become a priest in the temple like his father. Here we are aware that God can use anyone of any age who is called to be his servant. God gives one the spirit and the power and the fire in the belly. Jeremiah had to prophesy to the people and he knew they would not listen and would sadly go into captivity. He is called the weeping prophet.

Chapter 24

GOD'S GUIDANCE AND MIRACLES

Almost on a weekly basis my wife Sharon and I get into a conversation about our life, our children and our friends. We did that today, June 26th, 2013. We took a few minutes to reflect on the Lord's leading our lives up to this point. We think back on my life, how God led me along. We see his hand at work every step of the way with my first marriage to Dorothy, her death, and then my second marriage to Sharon. God used Sharon to help my young son Dyer and I out of our loss and depression. When our children Curtis and Joy were born we sent them off in the summers to Dyer and his wife Beth's home to help them all bond together. Then we thought of our friends, Angelo and Corrine, then Howard and Chris Redman, and finally our dear everlasting friends, Don and Kay Bennett. God brought these important people into our lives each at the right time. This is just another way for us to "Praise The Lord." It is important and heartwarming to take time to count your blessings of family and friends. To reflect on God's hand in guiding our lives.

I would like to say a word or two to our young people today. If God is speaking to your heart about following him and becoming his disciple, obedience is better than sacrificing a missed opportunity. Believe me in that you will know the Lord is speaking to you. His Holy Spirit will captivate your mind and soul. Follow his lead and you will not be disappointed. Be an avid reader and study those who have taken that step of obedience to Jesus Christ. Devour God's Word, meditate on it day and night. His Holy Spirit will lead you into the fullness of blessings. Another important read is Bonhoeffer's book, *The Cost of Discipleship*. Only the obedient believe and only those who believe are obedient. Study the life and ministry of St. Paul; "Follow me as I follow Christ."— 1 Corinthians 11:1 True righteousness begins with obedience.

Does God perform miracles that are beyond our cerebral and natural comprehension? Can God step in and momentarily suspend the laws of nature to comply with his destined will? What do you think? What is a miracle? I just finished reading C.S. Lewis on miracles. He makes an interesting observation; "The first thing to get clear in talking about miracles, whatever experiences we may have, we shall not regard them as miracles as miraculous if we already hold a philosophy which excludes the supernatural. We can always say we have been the victims of an allusion." C.S. Lewis continues, "Let us make no mistake. If the end of the world appeared in all the literal trappings of the Apocalypse, if the modern materialist saw with his own eyes the heavens rolled up and the great white throne appearing, if he had the sensation of being himself hurled into the lake of fire, he would continue forever, in the lake itself, to regard his experience as an illusion and to find the explanation of it in psycho-analysis, or cerebral pathology."

Do you believe in miracles? In 1980 at the Olympics we witnessed what many people called a miracle. The United States hockey team made it to the finals by beating other countries to face the Soviet Union team. The Russian players were always at their best and it was assumed that the USA team could not win the gold medal. The USA team had very young players. They were considered a long-shot; a super underdog. The Russians were seasoned professional. All they did day in and day out was play hockey. Hockey is Russia's national game. To the surprise of everyone including the Russians, USA put up a scrappy battle. The final quarter arrived and the teams were tied. For the first time in years the USA had a chance to beat the Russians. The crowd in the arena that day and in the entire United States TV audience went wild. All TVs were focused on our team. *Could it be possible? Could it be a miracle on ice?* Yes, Team USA won the gold medal! That was over 30 years ago and today we still talk about it as a 'Miracle on Ice.'

We heard in 2010 about the Chilean miners trapped two thousand feet below the surface in a mine cave-in. Bibles were sent down to them through a shaft of light. When they were rescued after being over 2,000 feet below ground for over 69 days miner Alberto Avalos exclaimed "This is a miracle from God." Another survivor said, "We have information that gives us hope."

Everyone who follows Christ has more than hope and faith because of God's promises, his Word that Speaks to us today. Colossians 1:27: "It is Christ in you the hope of glory." Hebrews 6:19 tells us: "This hope we have as an anchor to the soul." The authority with the Father that began in heaven is the same authority that his Spirit has to give to all who believe in Jesus Christ. When Jesus said good bye to his disciples as he departed into heaven, he said: " It is important that I go to be with my Father, the helper, (Gk. word 'paraclatos'), means encourager, comforter, one who stands beside us), the Holy Spirit, my Father will send in My name, he will teach you all things, and bring to your remembrance all that I have told you."—John 14:26: God has never stopped speaking to us for even a second. He is as near as your breath.

I can tell you on the basis of my own life of 85 years that I know the Word of God is living, that his VOICE is ALIVE. (Hebrews 4:12) It is not a dead book. The VOICE of God is living in my heart and running through my veins. Believe in the Lord Jesus Christ and you will be saved, both you and your household. I have been set on fire for God and his Word. I am God's kindling; on fire for God.

Chapter 25

GOD'S VOICE IN THE NEW TESTAMENT

G od's VOICE and that of Jesus Christ speak through the Holy Spirit: When we come to the New Testament the references to the Holy Spirit are even more numerous. The word for Spirit is pneuma (Gk), and is found in two hundred and sixty one passages. When Joseph was told to put Mary away the angel of the Lord reminded him (again his VOICE), "be not afraid to take Mary as your wife, for that which is conceived in her is of the Holy Spirit."—Matthew 1:20. Father Joseph accepted the answer because he knew enough about biology and the laws of nature. When the disciples saw Jesus walking on water, they were frightened because they understood the laws of nature. They knew something extraordinary was happening. When Jesus was at the wedding feast and changed the water into wine he again suspended the laws of nature. Yet again, Jesus fed the five thousand hungry people with two loaves of bread and five fishes. (Matthew 14:17)

John the Baptist is the forerunner of Jesus Christ; he was sent from God. John 1:6: "When Mary came to the house of Zacharias and Elizabeth, she heard Mary had arrived and her baby leaped in her womb; and she was filled with the Holy Spirit." Luke 1:40-41: "Zacharias is filled with the Holy Spirit. (Vs. 67) John is chosen by God while still in his mother's womb. He is given his name before he is born. (Vs.60-61). There was no one who had this name among his relatives. Here is the sovereign will of God being carried out. As a young man John goes forth to preach repentance and baptism.

JESUS IS GIVEN THE SAME DIVINE POWER AS THE FATHER: Jesus is given the same divine power and authority over all things. He healed the blind man, caused the lame to walk, and raised the dead. He is omniscient, omnipotent and omnipresent. He said: "The Son can do nothing of Himself, but only what He sees the Father do. He is subordinate to the Father's will."—John 5:19. Philip was very curious when Jesus told him: "He who has seen Me has seen the Father."—John 14:8-10. "I AM in the Father and the Father is in Me." Jesus does nothing unless the Father approves of it first. This is the unity and diversity of the Trinity.

Let's look at the meaning in the Bible of the word 'POWER.' We understand this word is used indiscriminately in the English language to mean a powerful person, a powerful message, the president has power, your words are powerful, there is power in his hands, you are powerfully strong and so on and on. We must remind ourselves even if we don't want to admit it that Satan has power. That is very evident starting with Genesis 1. He is the ruler of darkness and deception. He ever desires to undo God's work in the world, but ultimately he is a defeated foe. Jesus said: (his VOICE) "ALL POWER, (Greek word for dynamite), all powerful God, is given to Me in heaven and on earth."—Matthew 28:18 In his hands is the power to save, to heal and to pass judgment. Through his resurrection he has power over life and death.

Satan is a liar from the beginning. He masquerades as an angel of light but darkness and deception follow his every act in this world. People have difficulty believing this. Why? Even here he distracts us from the truth as he did in the Garden. We see his lies in bad contracts, people who promise one thing and do the opposite. We witness Satan's deception from the top in politics all the way down to bottom of the ladder. Politicians promise jobs, security and safety but instead prove full of perfidy. Satan whispers in our ear "DO IT! DO IT! DO IT!" On the opposite end is the truth and promises of God who enables us to resist and have victory over the devil. When will we look to God who keeps his promises? God says that if you seek me with all your heart and soul you will find me. Read Romans 10:9,10; John 1:1-4, 8-10. "He is the Lord God Almighty ("El Shadi), God all sufficient, God of the mountains."—Gen. 17:1-3.

The kings of Israel had enormous power and often their power was misused. The Hebrews never referred to the word 'God,' because his Word was so sacred and powerful. In the Old Testament metaphorically the term 'power' applied to God as "my strong tower, my mighty rock and my fortress."—Psalm 18:2 In the New Testament we have the Greek word 'dynamos' meaning power, acts of power (miracles); God is the source of all power. Jesus told his disciples: "…you will see the Son

of Man seated at the right hand of The Power, God." —
Mark 14:62 The Holy Spirit has this same power. Jesus
said when he comes upon the disciples they will receive
this power. *Mounce's Complete Expository Dictionary
of Old & New Testament Words* has 5 columns devoted
to 'power.' God used 'power' many times in the Bible.
(I Kings 15:23; 16:5,27; I Sam. 2:31; Matt. 26:64; Luke
5:17; I Corinthians 1:24. to name a few).

I have taught a class for on the New Testament book
of Hebrews. This book includes many incidents going
back to the Old Testament relative to Jewish history. It
too reveals God's workings with his people. The writer
discusses Jewish laws, the priesthood, rituals and sacrifices required under the old covenant. He moves forward to show how Jewish history ties in with the New
Testament covenant and its fulfillment in Jesus Christ,
God's Son became human, took on all our guilt and
sin and fulfilled the law and the sacrifices in himself
on the cross. Jesus Christ is our High Priest, redeemer
and savior and is seated at the right hand of the Father
ready to make intercession on behalf of all who believe.
(Hebrews 7:24) His priesthood is permanent, forever,
therefore: "He is able to save forever those who draw
near to God through Him, since He always lives to make
intercession for them..." — Hebrews 7:22-28. He is our
savior, sanctifier, healer and coming King.

Under the Old Covenant there were many priests.
They had to be appointed by God, set apart. The sons
of Aaron were chosen to be priests. They were responsible to perform the daily offering of sacrifices for sins
and prayers for the people. They represented the people
here on earth. Their work was never done. They must be

faithful in all their duties. It is estimated that the priests were in charge of completing over six hundred different steps in their work. It required a lot of help.

The Priests performed all the Jewish festivals and once a year the High Priest offered sacrifices for sin, took the blood of the lamb and entered the Holy of Holies and sprinkled it on the mercy seat. When a billow of cloud was observed over the Holy place God's presence verified that he was pleased. Now, under the New Covenant we have Jesus Christ the final, Priest King. He is the final sacrifice for sin. Following the destruction of the Temple in 70 A.D. sacrifices were no longer offered. In the book of Hebrews we learn that Jesus Christ is superior to angels, Moses, the tabernacle priesthood and the law. The Israelites suffered severe persecution and the trials of life. It was a time that many of the people were ready to throw in the towel. Here is an example of the righteous suffering with the wicked. We are to be strong, steadfast and resolute in our trust of Christ.

The Hebrew writer encourages the people to hold fast the faith they had received from the beginning. In the Old Covenant we read where God spoke in many ways through the prophets and in his last days he speaks through his only begotten Son, Jesus Christ, who is the author and finisher of our faith. The Holy Spirit is sent by Jesus Christ to encourage us to hold fast to our faith. Jesus Christ became one of us, took on all our sins in his body and voluntarily went to the cross, was crucified, dead, buried and rose from the dead to bring us new life and hope and we look to him and believe and are saved forever. One writer put it like this:

Jesus replies-
"I will leave my place and
I will come to your place, and
I will take your place so that
I can bring you to my place."

How did sin enter into the world? Romans 5:12: "... through one man, Adam, sin entered into the world, and death through sin, and so death spread to all men, for all have sinned." "But God demonstrated His love for us. In that while we were yet sinners, Christ died for us."—Romans 5:8

The writer of Hebrews addresses three different types of people in the world: In the first group are those who have turned from Judaism to follow Christ, their Messiah. These are people who heard Jesus speak, listened to his words and believed his message and were baptized. They witnessed his miracles and were amazed at his teaching, for he taught as one who had authority. They believed he was the Son of God.

The second group heard the same message, observed his miracles and signs. They admitted he must come from God but they held back. They wanted more signs and miracles. They were on the fence but not ready to take a stand either way. They were the doubters, the agnostics. To them James says, "a double minded man is unstable in all his ways."—James 1:8 The scribes and the Pharisees trusted their fate to the law.

The third group remained unimpressed with Jesus, his claims and his miracles. They were of their fathers Abraham, Isaac and Jacob. They admitted he had unusual powers and spoke with authority but they could not forget his father was Joseph the carpenter. They believed that their prophets

spoke of a Messiah who would come and free them from Roman oppression. They believed when he came he would set up his Kingdom to rule here on earth. They considered themselves the 'True Israel.' Jesus later said to them,

"Woe unto you scribes and Pharisees, leaders of the blind, whitened sepulchers, dead men's bones"— Matthew 23:13-33 (The deadly Woes.)

WHICH GROUP DO YOU BELONG TO?

Chapter 26

THE VOICES OF THE NEW TESTAMENT GOSPELS

The whole purpose of this book is to help people understand the Bible in a deeper way. As one writer puts it—"to encounter the timeless truth of God's Word as a compelling, life-changing reality." God's Word is a "kindle," a holy fire burning with love for you. It is God's voice.

In the New Testament we have four Gospels of Matthew, Mark, Luke and John (the beloved), each telling the story of Jesus Christ and his ministry as they witnessed it here on earth. In the background one can see the Holy Spirit at work in each gospel. Each writer gives us a little different perspective on the life of Jesus here on earth. The Gospels compliment each other. They formed a harmony, a symphony that encapsulated the full story of Jesus' life.

MATTHEW

Levi, later to be named Mathew, was a tax collector. He was called by Jesus to follow him. Wow, a tax collector. Ha! Today that would probably not be our choice. What relationship does a tax collector have with fishermen? Complete opposites. Mathew tells us about Jesus' life from a Jewish point of view. Here he traces the genealogy of Christ all the way back to Adam. Jesus is the Messiah King of Israel. His message is directed to the Jewish nation. Mathew was proficient in his use of the Greek language prevalent at the time. He was an eyewitness to Jesus Christ. I Chronicles 2:1-15: "Here is Jesus the promised Messiah. Here is the tax collector who left everything to follow Christ." He was one of the twelve Apostles. (Mark 3:18;Luke 6:15; Acts 1:13).

MARK

Mark was a close companion of the Apostle Peter. His Gospel was written in parallel with Matthew and Luke. Mark's Gospel is much shorter, right to the point. He presents Jesus as the authoritative Son of God, servant among men. (Mark 12:1, 8:27). Mark reaches out to the Roman and Gentile audiences. He leaves out genealogies found in Matthew and Luke. Mark presents Jesus as the suffering savior, the servant among men. He presents the human side of Jesus' life. He makes it clear that Christ came to seek and to save the lost. His mission was to fulfill the Father's promise. John Mark was a companion of Peter and cousin of Barnabas. (Col.4:10) This Gospel was written around A.D. 67-68. (see Acts 12:12, 25, 15:37). Mark's mother lived in Jerusalem. Mark developed slowly in his faith but later grew and became strong. (II Tim. 4:11) Mark appealed to the Roman mind.

LUKE

Luke was the physician who is also credited for writing the book of Acts. He reveals the descent of Jesus going back to David the King and back to Adam. It was written sometime in the 60's A.D. Luke, the only Gentile, was the only one to pen the scriptures from a Gentile perspective. He was a native of Antioch (Eusebius) and a companion of Paul. (Col. 4:14). The book of Acts centers on Antioch. In Acts 15:9 Luke dedicated his work to 'most excellent Theophillus' meaning the lover of God, or one whom God Loves.

Luke was not an eyewitness to all that Jesus did but his writings came from those who were eyewitnesses. Dr. Luke knew how to keep reliable and accurate records of Jesus' life, his miracles and his teachings. He presents Jesus Christ as the Great Physician, healer of the sick, with compassion for the lowly and the outcasts of Israel and society. (5:31,32; see 3:23-38; I Chron. 1:1-4, 24-28)

JOHN

John's writings are called 'the all by itself Gospel,' not connected to the synoptic Mathew, Mark and Luke. He declares Jesus Christ as Divine Son of God, Son of Man, Savior, Messiah. John 1:14-17: "And the Word, (Gk. Logos) became flesh and tabernacled among us, and we gazed upon his glory as an only One (begotten of the Father) full of grace and truth." The Greek translation makes it clear that Jesus Christ is the Word; also mentioned in John 1:1. He is the only one, the unique person who comes to us from the Father, sent by the Father to take on humanity, to become sin for us, who knew no sin that we might become the righteousness of God through his shed blood on the cross.

John speaks of the pre-existence of Christ. In John 6:29ff. are the "I AM's" of Christ. John's Gospel is called a spiritual gospel. John 14-17 tells more about the work of the Holy Spirit than the Synoptic books. It is in John 14-17 chapters where we learn how the ministry of the Holy Spirit affects all our lives. Jesus Christ makes it clear why he is sending the Holy Spirit into the world as every Christian has access to the Holy Spirit. The Holy Spirit is our teacher, our comforter, and our guide through life. He glorifies the Father and the Son.

John compliments the three other Gospels. John is the most theological Gospel, referring to God, the Son and the Holy Spirit as a divine unity. Jesus is the Word, the first and the last Word. He presents the witness of the Holy Spirit. (3:23- 14:16,17,26) John explains why all these things are written about Jesus. (according to the MacArthur Study Bible in John 20:31-320 the word 'believe' occurs over 100)

NICODEMUS

The description of the conversion experience of Nicodemus is in John 3. Nicodemus is the High Priest who went to see and speak with Jesus under the cover of night. Why? It may have been because of his rank as a ruler of the Jews, belonging to the Sanhedrin, a Pharisee. He had an intellect of power and esteem. He did not want to be seen associating with Jesus. He took a great risk to secret his visit. The Pharisees had nothing to do with Jesus Christ, this false teacher claiming to be the Messiah, Son of God. They proclaimed him to be a blasphemer.

Nicodemus is an example of a brilliant intellectual leader who does not understand the spiritual elements of God because he does not have the Spirit of God dwelling in his heart. His life was lived strictly by the Law. Nicodemus recognized Jesus as one who speaks (his Voice) with authority. He heard what others were saying through the rumors and grapevine. Nicodemus decided to check out this person who claimed to be from God. When they met he said to Jesus, "Rabbi, no one can do the things you do unless he comes from God." Nicodemus knew the law and the prophets that spoke of the day that would come for the Messiah's appearance. But Jesus responded with "You must be born again." That statement caught Nicodemus completely off guard. He didn't understand what Jesus was commanding. "Are there two births?" Nicodemus asked. "Can a man enter his mother's womb a second time and be born again?" Nicodemus understood what a first birth meant but did not understand a second spiritual birth. Jesus, of course, was talking about being born spiritually; the second birthing.

Jesus speaks (his VOICE), "…a person must be born of water and the Spirit, or he cannot enter the Kingdom of Heaven; that which is born of the flesh is flesh that which is born of the Spirit is Spirit."—John 3:5,6. The new birth involves a spiritual transformation from above. It is the Holy Spirit that enters a person's life. He transforms that life in Jesus Christ. Jesus gained Nicodemus' undivided attention. Jesus says "Truly, Truly" several times as it is imperative that he makes Nicodemus understand that the Spirit is the new life one receives when he/she accepts Jesus Christ into their hearts.

Water is sometimes referred to as the Word of God, so we water our life with the Word. Water quenches the thirsty soul. It speaks of cleansing and purifying. Fire and wind are also mentioned in the Bible. Refiner's fire purifies the soul. The breath of God moves with the wind. Both of these are mentioned in the Bible several times. This can only happen when one is born of the Spirit. Did Nicodemus get the message? It looks like he did because he took part in Jesus' burial.

In the New Testament Jesus Christ walked and talked personally with his Disciples and Apostles. They listened to his VOICE and also the VOICE of the Father. He came to seek and to save that which was lost (at the fall). He came not to be ministered to, but to minister and to give His life a ransom for many.

What did the disciples and the crowd witness?

THEY WITNESSED HIS VOICE IN ACTION. They witnessed his Words (his VOICE). "All power (authority) is given unto Me in heaven and in earth."—Matthew 28:18 HIS LIFE WAS A LIVING TESTAMONY TO HIS WORDS. His 'power' was not the power to blow up rocks or buildings, but power to save, to heal the sick, to raise the dead, to set at liberty those who are bruised. This was not power to destroy but to heal the broken hearted. Jesus sustains ALL things by the Word of his power. (Hebrews 1:3). His Father in heaven has given him all power. From this the assembled Church has all power to be obedient to Christ. (I Corinthians 5:4). "When the Son of man comes, He will come with much power and glory."—Matthew 24:30; II Thessalonians 1:7 "…with power and great glory in the Holy Spirit."—Luke 4:14.

THEY WITNESSED HIS WALK. He walked the walk and talked the talk. He called the Twelve Disciples to him, (Mark 3:13). He taught them and then he sent them out two by two into the world to proclaim his message. These were ordinary men, fishermen and tent makers. They witnessed his death, burial and resurrection. When C.S. Lewis was asked about Christianity he said if you want to start a new religion, raise someone from the dead. More than 500 people witnessed Christ being alive following the resurrection. Mary and Martha were the first. They found the huge stone rolled away from the tomb. The angel told them: "He is not here but is raised."—Mark 16:6-7 Jesus Christ is the only person who ever died and rose from the dead.

THEY WITNESSED HIS POWER TO HEAL AND RAISE THE DEAD. Jesus raised Lazarus from the dead after he had been in the tomb for four days and decomposition had already begun, but he died again. Going back to few verses in John we read where Jesus is talking to Martha. He said: (his VOICE) "I AM the resurrection and the life, he who believes in Me shall live even if he dies, and everyone who lives and believes in Me shall never die. Do you believe this?" Martha said: "I believe."— John 11:1-44

The Lazarus resurrection event gave witness to the disciples. Martha, Mary and others who were present verified the deity of Jesus Christ. The resurrection increased the faith of everyone and signaled his going to die on the cross. No one ever dared to make this statement: "I AM the resurrection and the life." There is only one person who could and would back it up. Now, my question to you is *who raised Jesus from the dead?*

God the Father Almighty did it. The righteousness of
God had to be satisfied. God could not look on sin. There
had to be a sinless offering for sin. The unrighteous-
ness of man had to be eradicated, but man could not do
this. God's Son was God's gift to the world. (John 3:16)
Jesus conquered death, hell and the grave. (I Corinthians
15:55-58) Man could not have faked this truth, though
they tried. Theoretically if Jesus Christ had not raised
from the dead by God the Father, Christianity should
have died. In I Cor. 15: 3-6 Paul warns: "…if Christ be
not raised from the dead we are of all men most miserable, our preaching is vain our faith is vain and we are
yet in our sins. But praise be to God He is risen." When
Jesus Christ speaks his Words and people listen, lives
are changed forever.

There would be no evangelism- the good news,
There would be no reaching out TO THE WORLD

BUT, we can shout, praise be to God for his unspeakable gift, Jesus Christ. God will either lead you by the
hand or with a bit in your mouth. The choice is yours.
What is the end for which God created you?

In my lifetime of almost eighty-five years I have read
many books written by some of the best writers who
ever lived. I have four hundred of them in my personal
library and I have one hundred-forty on my Kindle. I
broke up the library I had in California when we moved
to Buffalo, Minnesota and gave over five hundred volumes to Simpson University in Redding, California.
Many volumes I go back to read again and again. They
inspire me to live on and stay close to the Lord. They

encourage me to love my family and close friends, and to live an exemplary life before them and pray for them every day in my special hour of prayer. They encourage me to love God with all my heart, to worship and serve him always, and listen to his VOICE.

Chapter 27

"I AM THE GOOD SHEPHERD"

O ne of the most important characteristics of Jesus is his practicality. He says what he means to say and then explains it. In John chapter 10, Jesus declares to his disciples and to the world that in fact he is the Good Shepherd. Who doesn't know something about sheep? The Christmas story tells about the Wise Men in the fields tending their sheep. In driving across the farmlands of America we often see sheep grazing. This story is so relevant to our life. (The same imagery appears in Matthew 9:36; Mark 6:34; 14:27; Luke 15:1-3)

Most assuredly if he said it you can be sure it will happen. He confirms there is only one door for the sheep to walk through and everyone who crosses its threshold is safe and secure. If anyone tries to climb up some other way they are known to be imposters. The true sheep (believers) hear his VOICE and the doorkeeper opens the door for them to come in. " The sheep hear his VOICE and he calls his own sheep by name."—John 10:27-28 The true shepherd goes before his sheep and his sheep follow Him. FOR THEY KNOW HIS VOICE. They will not listen to the voice of a stranger but flee from him. In the Western world sheep dogs are used to drive the sheep responding to their master's commands. It is said that Eastern shepherds have their own unique call that their sheep recognize, for they know their shepherd's voice. He calls each one by name.

A Story: We Enter Through the Right

We all have had the experience of following directions, going to the right building, the right floor and the right room number. Somehow, sometimes we get all mixed up and miss our appointment. We must have entered through the wrong door? Best, to start over again. Jesus uses many such illustrations to help us understand his directions. If we ignore or deny his directions and truths we must face the consequences of disbelief.

The Pharisees were so locked into their legal system of do's and don'ts they were blinded to the truth and completely ignored the Old Testament message of the prophets and the Word of God. They wore their phylactery on their foreheads filled with scripture verses. They wore garments that brought attention to themselves as they stood on street corners. They wanted all to see and hear them as they openly proclaimed Jesus was sent from the devil. They called him a blasphemer.

Jesus was speaking with power from God and the Holy Spirit. Therefore they were actually condemning themselves—by your words you are justified and by your words you condemn yourself. Jesus is the Shepherd and the only door whereby followers may come to the Father in heaven. God's promised salvation is in his Son. No other door is open. As John MacArthur interprets the Gospel of John: "Only Jesus Christ is the one true source for the knowledge of God and the one basis for spiritual security." (John 10:9-10) Jesus Christ is the Good Shepherd and he will take care of his sheep. Their security rests with his promises for eternal life. He has the power to keep them safe. Once under his care no one or anything can harm us. He alone has sovereign control of all things. (Romans 8:29-39)

Chapter 28

SPEAKING THROUGH THE ACTS
OF THE APOSTLES

In the New Testament a better title for the Acts book
is 'The Acts of the Holy Spirit through the Apostles.'
The Holy Spirit is the third Person of the Trinity. The
Holy Spirit was responsible in directing all the guidance and ministry that the Apostles carried out. The day
of Pentecost had arrived. It is the seventh Sunday after
Easter that celebrates the descent of the Holy Spirit. It
is also the fiftieth day after Passover. (Webster's New
Word Dictionary)

During the period when Jesus was with the disciples they were with him on a daily basis. They heard
his VOICE speaking over and over again and they
became very familiar with his teachings as he spoke (his
VOICE), as the One with power and authority. The Holy
Spirit was with him and ministered to him. When it came
time for his departure he told them to wait a few days;
ten in all. He returned and met them where they were
praying. He breathed upon them and they received the

Holy Spirit. The symbol of the Holy Spirit is breath, fire, wind and water. Remember what Jesus told (his VOICE), Nicodemus in John 3: "the wind blows where it wishes and you hear the sound thereof, but do not know where it came from or where it is going; so is everyone who is born of the Spirit."

I would like to mention several books I have been reading; *The American Standard Version of the Bible on Acts; The Book of Acts* by F.F. Bruce, and *The Life of St. Paul by Pope Benedict XVI* (outstanding Roman Catholic scholar). The above writers share important information about Paul's life. He was born approximately around the year 8 A.D. He was born in Tarsus, Cilicia (Acts 22:3, 25-28). It is said that Tarsus was the place where Antony and Cleopatra met. Paul was caught between three cultures, Greek, Roman and Jewish. He learned the trade of tent making. As was the custom every Jewish boy by age twelve was confirmed in the Bar Mitzvah. He went to Jerusalem to receive his education under the tutelage of Rabbi Gamaliel, nephew of the great Rabbi Hillel. Here he received the strictest teaching of the Pharisees, the Mosaic Torah. (Gal.1:4)

The Apostle Paul was a religious zealot. He became incensed when he heard about Jesus of Nazareth, who was becoming a threat to Jewish Orthodoxy. Therefore, he proudly set out to persecute the church of God. (I cor. 15:9; Gal. 1:13; Phil. 3:6). Paul could not see beyond the Law and the Torah. This is the reason he set out for Damascus. It was while he was on the road that he met his Maker. Here we see the transformation of Saul/Paul from earthly man to heavenly servant of God, the Holy Spirit intervening.

Following his miraculous conversion Paul set out on three missionary journeys. Paul and Barnabas sailed together on their first journey (Acts 13) Then Paul and Silas set out on the second journey (Acts 15-18). The third journey began in Antioch (Acts 18:23-21:16). Here we encounter the Church of the Gentiles and it was in Antioch that the name 'Christian' was coined. Then Paul traveled to Ephesus, where he stayed for two years. Later on he would be taken as a prisoner to Rome. House churches were established along the way, all recorded in the book of Acts. Here we have the beginnings of the Church of the Gentiles. Certain religious practices under Judaism such as circumcision had to be cleared up because now all who believed and accepted Jesus Christ received the circumcision of the heart.

God still stops us in our tracks with his VOICE today. Anytime, anyplace he chooses. Paul is a perfect example of this. Be thankful if he stops you. Don't miss his call. In my lifetime it is very clear that unless God calls a person to be saved, it will never happen. He is sovereign in all circumstances. Jesus said: "No one comes to the Father except by me."—John 14:6 In the New Testament we read the story of the Apostle Saul/Paul. In the book of Acts, Chapter 7, he describes the predicament man is caught in (remember, he was spiritually blind before his conversion).

Even with all the miracles they witnessed Jesus' own people rejected him and struggled with his truth and life. Why? They believed in a Messiah who would one day come and rescue them from the Romans and set up his kingdom here on earth. They could not believe he suddenly appeared without their knowledge. They were

173

still stuck, attached to the law and sacrificial ceremonies going back to the time of Moses. As a Pharisee Saul/ Paul knew the law frontward and backward, he was very wise and intelligent. No one broke the law where he was concerned. He heard of this so-called new teacher of the Jews who claimed to be the Messiah. Many people believed his message. Paul determined to find who these believers were and bring them back to trial. Paul was working in his own strength convinced the Law must be kept at all costs.

The Apostles would continue to devote themselves to prayer and the ministry of the word. (Acts 1: 1-6). This scripture is the basis of qualification of leadership and ministry in the church for elders, deacons, and all church leaders. Ephesians adds that they are to be the husband of one wife, manage their own household and not be greedy. They are to have a good reputation and are full of the Holy Spirit. In far too many instances I have found churches paying very little attention to the importance of the Holy Spirit. This means they ignore this aspect of God's work or they have never read it or they think it is unnecessary. And the results prove it. I recommend they saturate themselves in the chapters 14-17 of John.

Right here I would like us to pause and listen to John, chapter fourteen, the most powerful and beautiful statement that Christ gave his worried disciples about life and faith. In these verses we listen to his VOICE: "Let not your heart be troubled: you believe in God, believe also in me. In my Father's house are many mansions: if it were not so, I would have told you. I go to prepare a place for you. And if I go and prepare a place for you, I will come again, and receive you to myself; that where I am, there you may be also." This is his promise guaranteed. Then in verse 27 he says: "Peace I leave with you, my peace I give unto you; not as the world gives, give I unto you. Let not your heart be troubled, neither let it be afraid."

This passage answers today's questions and fears— fear for today and fear of tomorrow. Jesus quenches these fears with two of the most important promises we all need today: we are troubled about many things and we do not have any real peace about where we are going or what is next in our world. When we turn our lives over to Jesus Christ we are assured we can stop worrying. Christ brings peace to the heart. Stop right now and ask Christ to save you and take charge of your life. "My peace I leave with you." Amen.

Back to Saul's problems: Saul was given letters from the High Priest of the Sanhedrin to capture anyone who followed 'the way.' He headed out on the road to Damascus and as he neared the city of Damascus a flash of light struck him and he fell to the ground blinded. A voice spoke out, "Saul, why are you striking out against Me?" Saul cried out, "…who art thou Lord?" Saul knows this voice is different. He rises to his feet and is led into the city. He is told to meet with a man called Ananias who will tell you what you must do. Going ahead of Saul, the angel of the Lord spoke to Ananais to prepare him to receive Saul. Ananais had heard of Saul's mission to arrest the followers of Jesus. He was scared to meet Saul until the angel assured him would be safe.

Ananias–laid his hands on Saul/Paul and he received his sight back and was filled with the Holy Spirit. Ananias laid his hands on Saul/Paul on the authority of the Holy

Spirit. (Acts 9:17). Saul's name changed to Paul. The scales fell off his eyes and immediately he was baptized. Paul was transformed and spent some time in prayer waiting on the Lord before he set out to be Christ's disciple. Later he was stoned and left for dead. He was put in prison for his following Christ. Later he paid the full price with his life in death.

What does it mean to lay the hands on someone? I was ordained under the Christian and Missionary Alliance, at our General Conference meeting. The District Superintendent with several pastors called me forward and they laid their hands on me and dedicated me to the Lord's work. But the Lord had already called me. This was my ordination verse:

"You did not choose Me, but I chose you and appointed you that you should go and bear fruit and that your fruit should abide, so that whatever you ask the Father in My name, He may give it to you." —John 15:19

In my ministry over the years I have formed the habit of laying my hand on a person's shoulder. I do it subconsciously. Why? Whenever I see someone hurting or in need of encouragement what should we do? Offer not only our prayers but if possible, offer our hand. Jesus Christ would do that. (John 15:9). It seems natural for me to do that. I also like to give people hugs. At first some people are shy but I have found most people enjoy it. Why? It is my way of encouraging people, of saying quietly, *may God bless you*. Hopefully, it's letting them know I care.

Chapter 29

"I FELT THE WIND AT MY BACK"

I n our retirement years Sharon and I have started reading and sharing books together. We come home from our walk at the gym and she puts on a pot of coffee, we sit and Sharon reads to us. My wife and I are reading a book about Dr. David Levy entitled *Gray Matter: A Neurosurgeon Discovers the Power of Prayer...One Patient at a Time* by David Levy and Joel Kilpatrick. David Levy is a Jewish doctor, head neurological (brain) surgeon at a hospital in San Diego. He is one of the most outstanding people I have ever read. God has put his hand on this man's life in a unique and personal way. His struggle with his Christian witness and with his suffering patients is unbelievable. He had to decide whether in his profession if the ridicule he might receive from his peers by offering prayer and hope to his patients before going into brain surgery was more important than the personal repercussions he would endure. I want to share one of his stories. Dr. David Levy writes:

"As I began treating my own patient's instead of hypothetical patients in a classroom, I began to see my

own carefully honed surgical skills fail to produce the outcomes I expected. I had faith in surgery and had given many years of my life to acquiring the skills necessary to do the most difficult operations. I had thought that if I could do a procedure perfectly, I would get a perfect result every time. I was wrong. It was out of disappointment over bad outcomes that I began to appreciate the connection between our physical and spiritual lives. I was growing in my knowledge of God and beginning to respect the spiritual world in my personal life, though I still insisted that there was no place for it in the hospital, my opinion on that too, slowly began to change. The line between the two areas blurred, and my reasons for separating them began to crumble.

Empirical evidence confirms the connection. Studies have shown that approximately one in five patients (19 percent) want their physicians to pray with them on a routine office visit and only seven percent do not believe in the power of prayer. I could no longer ignore my impulse to offer patients more than just physical care, when there was much more to them than their bodies."

The thought process he goes through to make his decision to pray is worth reading by itself, and worthy of our attention. Dr. Levy goes on to describe all the ramifications he would face with his colleagues, friends and associates, were he to take prayer seriously. As a top neurological surgeon he would become personally vulnerable to scrutiny and opposition—"Through all my questions and doubts I felt an inner voice saying to me, 'If you are worried about being misunderstood, I can promise you that you will be. Jesus was. But you still need to do the right thing." I decided to ask the next patient, regardless of what might happen. When I prayed for the first person before surgery I placed my hand on her shoulder. I paused. Then I thought of whom we were talking to and not where we were. Out of nowhere, I felt a wind at my back, pushing me on. Without any foresight the prayer began to flow like a river cascading downhill."

"God you have been with Mrs xx since she was a baby. You know all about her vessels, and I know that you cam help me fix them, Please give me wisdom and skill. I ask for success in this surgery, in the name of Jesus, Amen."

The surgery was successful both physically and spiritually. You have to read *Gray Matter*. You owe it to yourself and your family to read this book. Dr. Levy experienced God's presence and power in his life.

In the Bible one of the manifestations of God is wind as the breath of God, The Holy Spirit guides the life of Paul. I challenge you to read Acts, chapter 9 for yourself. You decide? Could Paul have accomplished all that he did with only his own strength? Not hardly.

God's righteousness is in direct opposition to man's proclivity to sin culminating in disbelief. Man rejects the truth God has made perfectly clear from the beginning. Paul tells us God's eternal power and glory is clearly visible. (Romans 1:17f). Paul sends this letter to the churches in Rome though he has not had a chance to visit them yet. At this time he is a staunch follower of Christ. Paul wrote, "I am willing and eagerly ready to preach the Gospel to you also who are in Rome. For I am not ashamed of the Gospel (good news) of Christ; for it is

the power (Gk. dunamis–dynamite) working unto salvation (for deliverance from eternal death) to EVERYONE
WHO BELIEVES with a personal trust and a confident
surrender and from firm reliance, to the Jew first (his
people of Israel) and also to the Greek. It is the Gospel
of God's righteousness springing from faith."—Romans
1:16,17 Amplified N.T.

Does man's rebellion nullify the truth of God's
divinely inspired word? Not at all. In fact its witness
is even stronger than ever. Romans chapter 1: "...one
man's true freedom only comes when he begins listening
to what God says about his human predicament." Paul
found this out in time. Jesus gave strong words to those
who believed in him—"If you abide in My Word, then
you are truly disciples of Mine, and you shall know the
truth, and the truth shall set you free."—John 8:32,33.
In II Corinthians 5:7, we read: "For we walk by faith,
(that is we regulate our lives and conduct ourselves... in
relationship to God and divine things), for we walk by
faith not by sight."

Chapter 30

LET ME TELL YOU A FISH STORY

True fishermen love to fish though they know that whatever they catch has some bones. Most of us love the taste of fish, but because they have bones do we decide not to eat fish? Not usually, therefore, we gladly put the bones aside and enjoy the delicious fish. In the same way some people decide to reject the Bible because there are too many mysteries cannot be explain or do we accepted. What God has made perfectly clear to us in his Word is to put the bones—the mysteries—to the side until we get answers to our questions? There are some things about God we were never meant to know. These things are known only to God. But, even though some secrets remain God's alone he still wants us to know the Bible. Therefore to neglect the beautiful Bible teachings is to our own sorrow.

Most of the time we have just ignored the Bible because of what we have heard from others. We let the fear of the 'bones' take over. Let the Bible speak for itself. It needs no defense. I have been studying the Bible for sixty years. Do I know everything? NO! But I do have a good grasp of what God's will is for my life. Yes, and I pursue it daily with guidance from the Holy Spirit. Man keeps himself from knowing God personally because...

HE BELIEVES MORE IN HIS EXCUSES THAN IN GOD'S PROMISES.

Say the above statement over again and again until you understand it. Man's intellectual pride gets in the way...educated people don't believe in God. We may have witnessed 'so called Christians' and found them hypocritical and bigoted. Bright people don't waste their time on such fables and myths that is until they are suddenly stricken with a dreaded disease. When guilt and dread loom at the door you loose the control you had over your life up to that point. Dr. Levy talks about his experiences with skeptics: "The reason we feel guilty is because we are guilty. We are guilty of going against what we know is right. God calls it sin. The cure for guilt and sin is confession and forgiveness."

There is only one person who can forgive sin and that is the sinless One, Jesus Christ. If you hold strong doubts about the Bible ask yourself this question: Who wrote the Bible? Your doubts may sound like these... *Two people were involved, therefore it is a myth. God is a myth and it is a fictitious story made up to deceive people. God must be a charlatan.* Don't let intellectual pride get in the way.

One or two people could not have been so clever, plus with man's proclivity toward sin and disbelief would he want to tell a story that brings judgment upon his disobedience? Just because an atheist or an agnostic disbelieves the Bible does not mean it is untrue. In fact it may be truer than ever.

During Jesus' earthly ministry he was confronted time and time again about who was telling the truth by the Greeks, Romans, Pharisees, Sanhedrin, the synagogue and Pilot. The world today is asking the same questions as the ancient doubters. Jesus said: "I AM the way, the truth and the life no one can come to the Father but by me."—John 14:6.

Jesus in conversation with his disciples asked them *who do men say I AM?* The greatest question of all time, *who am I?* The disciples responded that people mistook Jesus for John the Baptist, Elijah, Jeremiah or one of the prophets. He said to them, "...but who do you say that I AM?" Simon Peter answered, "...you are the Christ, the Son of the living God." Jesus said, "...flesh and blood did not reveal this to you, but my Father who is in heaven"—Matthew 13-17. What other proof do we need? People who are always daydreaming look for signs in the sky. Theologian Dietrich Bonhoeffer asked himself this question *Who Am I?* His answer is in this poem: "Whoever I am thou knowest, O God, I am thine." He died a martyr's death.

Let's reexamine this—The prophet Isaiah says: "Come let us REASON together." If God is a myth then God doesn't exist and if God doesn't exist then man doesn't exist, he is a myth. The world doesn't exist. The sun, moon and stars don't exist; life on earth doesn't exist. The philosopher Renee Descartes said, "Cogito ergo sum."—I think, therefore I am. I am real after all. I am fully rational and intelligent. At first he began with the premise to doubt everything. Later his argument led to the ontological proof in the existence of God. We can conceive of a perfect being (God) therefore he must exist.

This is a good example of man trying to find God on his own outside divine revelation. To deny God is to doubt your own existence. Psalm 139: "God knows when I sit down and when I rise up...where can I go from your Spirit? Where can I flee from your presence...you form my inward parts; you did weave me in my mother's womb. I will give thanks to you, for I am wonderfully made... and my soul knows it very well."

Chapter 31

HOW DID THE SCRIPTURES COME TO US?

How did the Scriptures come to us? This is a valid question. The process of writing the 66 books of the Old and New Testaments covered a span of over 1400 to 1600 years. God took his time to reveal his plan for man's redemption following Adam and Eve's expulsion from the Garden. God chose to use people to tell his story. He used over forty different individuals to unfold God's progressive revelation. He revealed his plan a little at a time. At first it was through oral transmission. Holy men of old were moved by the Holy Spirit as they wrote down the words given to them by God. Listen to Hebrews 1:1-2: "In many separate revelations each of which set forth a portion of the Truth and in different ways God's voice spoke of old to our forefathers in and by the prophets. But in the last days His voice has spoken to us in the person of a Son, (Jesus Christ), whom He appointed Heir and lawful Owner of all things, also and through Whom He created the worlds and the reaches of space and the ages of time- that is, He made, produced, built, operated and arranged them in order." (the Amplified New Testament)

JESUS IS THE LANGUAGE OF GOD.
Jesus is the VOICE of God,
Jesus is God.

Listen to a few of these statements regarding the VOICE of God:

" Then a cloud formed, overshadowing them, and a VOICE came out of the cloud, "This is My beloved Son, listen to Him." All at once they looked around and saw no one with them, except Jesus."—Matthew 9:7; 8

"Truly, truly I say unto you, an hour is coming, and now is, when the dead will hear the VOICE of the Son of God, and those who hear (his VOICE) will live."—John 5:25 (the resurrection)

"So faith comes through hearing (his VOICE), and hearing by the word of Christ."—Romans 10:13

"Behold, I stand at the door and knock; if anyone hears My VOICE and opens the door, I will come in to him and will dine with him, and he with Me."—Revelation 3:20

Jesus told his disciples that he who has seen me has seen the Father also. Philip was confused and said, show us the Father and we will be satisfied. It is like asking for another sign. Now if Philip needed re-assurance about the Father and Jesus was right in front of him how much more proof is needed. "...Lord, help our belief turn to your truth. Believe and you will be saved."—John 14:11

Jesus uses the Greek formula "ego eimi (I AM) in several different places in the Gospels:

" I AM the bread of life. (6:35, 41, 48, 51),
"I AM the light of the world." (8:12)
"I AM the gate for the sheep." (10:7-9)
"I AM the good shepherd." (10:11, 14)
"I AM the resurrection and the life." (11:25)
"I AM the way and the truth and the life." (14:6)
"I AM the true vine." (15:1-3)
"Before Abraham was born, I AM." (8:58)
"I AM who I AM." Exodus 3:14

There is no doubt that *He is who He says He is.* "I AM" is how they were to recognize that he came from God. Jesus was identifying himself with God. All through the Gospels Jesus identifies himself with the Father. "I and my Father are One." "Whatever the Father does that is what I do." "I can do nothing of my own self." This identification and subordination of Jesus to the Father, making himself co-equal and co-eternal with God, is what set the priests, rabbis and scribes on fire. To them this was blasphemy. They could not see that he was the Messiah come in the flesh. They expected that when he came he would set up his throne here on earth and drive out Roman rule and persecution.

JESUS IS THE LANGUAGE OF GOD.
Jesus is the VOICE of God,
Jesus is God.

In saying this I mean Jesus was in complete control of his life. Jesus could lay it down (as a sacrifice for sin) and he could take it up (resurrected). Jesus and the Father are one. Jesus did nothing without the Father's approval. In the gospels he reminds his apostles over and over again of the unity he has with the Father. (John 14:10-18) As born again Christians we are admonished to do the same thing. Whatever we do is to the glory of God. We listen to the voice of the Holy Spirit who Christ sent to teach us and to guide us into all truth. He is our comforter and guide. We are not to sit idly on the fence; Christ has called us into the thick of the battle. Jesus did not leave us orphans. (John 14:16-18) This whole 14th chapter of John is a towering testimony to the relationship of the Father to his Son and the Son to the Holy Spirit.

Chapter 32

SPIRITUAL BOREDOM

D r. A.W. Tozer's in his book *And He dwelt Among Us: Teachings from the Gospel of John* talks about the 'Curse of Spiritual Boredom.' He says this occurs when Christians become addicted to the activity of the world around them to the exclusion of helpful spiritual disciplines. They become more interested in the world around them than the 'Eternal Word' within them. Spiritual boredom is the consequence of immaturity. Dr. Tozer writes: "Christians are easily bored with anything that is routine. They want to liven up life with excitement and activity whereas the Christian life should be nurtured by daily disciplines." "…To maintain a balance in the Christian life is the great secret of maturity. We are dying by degrees because we are resting in the truth of the Word and are forgetting that there is a Spirit of the Word without which the truth of the Word means nothing to the human spirit." We must ACT on what the Word teaches us. A double minded man is unstable in all his ways. The choice is ours. We need to be set on fire by allowing the Holy Spirit his rightful place in our hearts. Kindle the Holy Spirit.

In going through the study of the book of Hebrews we come to one of the most inspiring and profound passages in the Bible. It is one of the Scriptures that inspired me to name this book *More Than Just Words*. It is (Paraphrase) Amplified New Testament:

Hebrews 4:12:
For the Word of God Speaks, (it is the VOICE of God),
It is the Living Word, it is the Active Word.
It is Alive and full of Power, (Gk. Word for dynamite), it is not power to crush rocks or blow up buildings, it is power to save, to heal, power to give new life.
It is energizing and effective, it awakens the soul

Hebrews 4:13:
It is sharper than any two-edged sword, penetrating to the Dividing line of the soul, and the immortal Spirit,
It penetrates the joints and marrow, the deepest part of our
Nature, exposing and sifting, analyzing and judging the very thoughts and purposes of the heart.

Dr. A.B. Simpson in his book on the Holy Spirit writes that the sword of the Spirit represents the slaying power. It is the symbol of death and death is the deepest revelation of Christ's salvation. The grave is forever the symbol of the Gospel, and the cross means not only his death but ours too. Therefore Satan hated it, and tried to make Peter reject it. Therefore the sentence of death (Gk.thanatos) has passed upon all Adam's race. This is the work of the Holy Spirit, to put to death the life of sin and death. "O death, where is thy sting?" — 1 Corinthians 15:55-56 Romans 5:12: "Therefore, just as through one man's sin entered the world, and death through sin, and thus death passed to all men, because all sinned." Jesus did not come to bring peace, but a sword. (Matthew 10:34)

When Jesus Christ comes into a person's life everything changes for the BEST. The Holy Spirit verifies Jesus Christ is the truth and the life. Our lives are changed forever. "The earthly gives way to the heavenly that which is born of the flesh is of the flesh, that which is born of the Spirit is from God." — John 3:6 "...therefore as new born babes in Christ our world is moving in a different direction. Jesus said, "I AM the way, the Truth and the life, no one comes to the Father except by Me."(John 14:1,6; Romans 8).

Chapter 33

WHAT IS THE CHRISTIAN LIKE?

I t is for certain he/she is not what most people think or how some so called Christians act. God's Word says Christians are to be different.

- When a person receives Christ he/she is a new creation. We are the same people, same voice, same looks outside, but inside we are new people because now we follow Christ and his Word. Jesus put his seal upon us. We are his workmen called to follow and obey his calling. "You shall know the Truth and the Truth shall set you free."—John 8:32 We are truly free. By faith we have that peace that surpasses all understanding. Jesus said: "… peace I leave with you, My peace I give to you, let not your heart be troubled and don't let it be afraid."—John 14: 1-3 From now on he is in control.

- As his disciples we are to touch other lives for Christ. On the surface, it seems impossible for one to reach those who are not yet saved. This is where the Holy Spirit has to come and convince a person that God's Word is true. Then the Holy Spirit convinces them that God loves them and he sent his only begotten Son to save them. Spiritual things are spiritually discerned and without the Spirit of God you cannot understand the workings of God. Believe and you will be saved. He who comes to God must believe that God lives and that he rewards those who receive him.

- We dedicate ourselves to pray for our brothers and sisters whoever needs Christ. We pray for their health and safety and we love them even if they are seen as disobedient to the Lord. We remember, he first loved us while we were yet sinners. We are the Johnny Apple Seeds. We are called upon to sow the seed. Jesus Christ says, "...anyone who wishes to come after Me, let him deny himself, take up his cross and follow Me."— Matthew 16:21. He touched my life with his fire. In this world you will have tribulation, pain and suffering, but Jesus said be of good cheer, I have overcome the world.

- We are to live the life of the over comer, we are his disciplined disciples. We are called to fight the fight of faith for all our loved ones and to suffer for them if necessary. I never stop praying they will be awakened to God's truth. This calling of God is not just for pastors, teachers, evangelists and missionaries. Every person who has truly accepted Christ has a ministry to perform. The Holy Spirit is sent to help you find what it is. We are not saved to sit on the sidelines. We are not meant to sit on the sidelines and become locked in to TV or be narcissistic. We are meant to get involved in the battle for truth.

- You will recognize true Christians for their love for God, and each other, and the way they show love for strangers. We are still sinners, BUT we are progressively moving in the direction of following the call of Christ.

Chapter 34

FACE TO FACE WITH GOD

G od speaks his VOICE to Moses after he has led
three million out of Egypt. They sojourned in the
wilderness for 40 days and 40 nights. They were hot,
dusty and dirty from their long march. They complained
to Moses. God responded by quenching their thirst and
feeding their hunger. He has Moses strike a rock and
water spilled forth. Then God sent down quail and
manna from heaven to feed them. But this demonstra-
tion of God's caring miracles did not satisfy them. They
clamored for more and more. God became angry at all
their endless complaining. The Israelites responded by
hoarding the food. God never rewards people for being
disobedient. God sent serpents among them and many
died. For those who were sick and wanted to be healed
God told Moses to set up a serpent on a pole and all
who looked to it were healed. They exercised their will
to believe God could heal them. (Exodus 16:17th Ch.;
Numbers 21:6,9).

The children of Israel finally arrive at the Mountain
of God with Moses. Mount Sinai was quaking violently,

ablaze in fire because the Lord had descended upon it. Out of the chaotic landscape came the sound of a trumpet. Moses spoke and God answered with thunder. God called Moses to climb up the mountain. God reminded the Israelites again, "I AM the Lord your God, who brought you out of the land of Egypt, out of the house of slavery. You shall have no other gods before Me."— Exodus 20:1-3. God is a very jealous God and he gave them orders to obey his commands. Why? God knew the moment they took their eyes off of him they would be jealous of the nations surrounding them who worshiped other gods, images and idols of their own creation.

What was said in the face-to-face meeting of God and Moses? Did they discuss the Creation or perhaps was it a fatherly chat about God's promises to Abraham? It was a very long meeting and after many days and nights the Israelites feared Moses just wasn't going to return to lead them. Their leader was no longer with them so their patience and anxiety boiled over onto Aaron, the priest. Since Moses was gone they cried out to Aaron to make them a golden calf. Aaron, a coward, gave in to their demands even though he understood more about obedience to God than they did. Once the golden calf was set up they began to worship it and have a big party. God saw what was happening and sent Moses back down the mountain.

Once more they became obstinate and rebellious. Moses challenged Aaron and asked why he didn't stop it? His answer, "…you know the people yourself, that they are prone to evil."—Exodus 32: 21-23. It seems the Israelites worshiped Moses more than God. God saw what they were doing and in his anger was ready to destroy those who were involved. Moses entreated the Lord not to destroy them, and the Lord changed his mind. God calls Moses a second time to climb the Mountain again to receive the commandments that were destroyed in anger.

We need to take a good look at these stories from Exodus. What can we learn from them? These teachings are a mirror of ourselves and of our obstinate attitudes. We certainly are no different, man's nature and proclivity toward sin is the same today as in ancient times. We are just as rebellious as the Israelites. And like them we need redemption and as much help from God as they needed. Jesus Christ sent the Holy Spirit to be our advocate and guide. In Exodus we read time and time again that God has face-to-face conversations with Moses. In Ex. 33:11: "Thus the Lord used to speak to Moses FACE TO FACE just as man speaks to his friend." Again in Ex. 33:12,16,17: "I have known you by your name... you have found favor in My sight, and I have known you by your name."

These are examples of God speaking (God's VOICE) directly to Moses. No one has seen God and lived. But this certainly tells us that God knows us by our name. Read the Psalm 139. God gets very personal in both the Old and New Testament. The very hairs on our head are numbered. God knew us before we were born. Such statements as this boggle the mind. It is too much for our finite mind to comprehend therefore it is for us to accept.

Be face to face with God by listening to his Word. By your faith and trust believe in him. Stop trying to run and hide from God, run to him.

In studying the book of James this thought came to me. God will either lead you by the hand or with a bit in your mouth. Which will it be?

James talks about the fiery tongue that gets out of control and the negative consequences. In this sense I think of people I have known who fight God and resist his word. It is a long passage so let me abbreviate it. James 3:3-12 talks of how we put bits into horses mouths so they may obey us. The bit directs their entire body as well... This is similar to how great ships are driven by strong winds but their course is directed by a very small rudder at the command of the captain or pilot. The tongue, a small part of the body boasts great things...set on fire it defiles the entire body and sets a course for the one's entire life...with it we bless the Lord and Father and curse men made in the likeness of God...from the same mouth comes cursing and blessings. God wants to lead and direct our lives because he loves us with an everlasting love, but will we let him?

Moses was the constant intercessor for the Israelites. Many times we are surprised at those whom God chooses to use as his spokesperson; often they are the opposite of what we would personally choose. We have seen how God spoke (his VOICE), personally to different people at various times throughout the Old Testament. The Old Testament is full of the stories of many priests being slave to keeping strict laws and performing sacrifices for atonement for sin. They were locked into the law and keeping their rituals. Through their prophets they were looking for their Messiah Priest King. They could not bring themselves to believe Jesus was this Messiah they were expecting. Jesus fulfilled the law and the covenant promises by the shedding of his own blood on the tree. Therefore, since having a great High Priest, Jesus Christ, who passed down through the heavens, let us boldly come to the throne of heaven. Let us draw near with confidence to the throne of grace that we may receive mercy and find peace in our souls. (II Cor. 5:21)

In the New Testament Jesus Christ walked and talked with his apostles and disciples and delivered his Father's will in obedience and trust. They heard his VOICE and became spellbound with his message to take up the cross and follow him. Discipleship means obedience to his Word. We need to study carefully John chapters 14-17. Why? They will open our eyes to the great promises of God. English Christian evangelist and biblical scholar, Dr. Arthur W. Pink wrote Bible commentary on the Gospel of John. When he came to chapters 14-17 of John he wrote; "Here the Lord Jesus begins his Paschal Discourse, a discourse which for tenderness, depth and comprehensiveness is unsurpassed in all of Scripture. It was given to the Eleven on the last night before He died. It is likened to the glorious radiance of the setting sun, surrounded with dark clouds, and about to plunge into darker, which, fraught with lightening, thunder and tempest wait on the horizon to receive Him." This section of John's gospel is the most beautiful in the New Testament Bible. Knowing Jesus is about to enter one of death's darkest nights yet here we find the Savior's love for his own and the love of God poured out in one stroke after another. Instead of concentrating on what suffering and death awaits him, Jesus spends his last hours comforting the Eleven. Listen to vs.1; "Let not your heart be troubled, believe in God, believe also in Me." Then move to Vs. 27: "Peace I leave with you, my peace give to you, not as the world gives do I give to you. "Let not your heart be troubled, nor let it be fearful."

Let's break this down to simpler terms. In the world you will have tribulation...sooner or later we all find out that life is not a bowl of cherries. For some people suffering comes earlier, death of a child, financial difficulties, divorce because the wife does not get enough love and support or the husband does not receive proper respect for who he is. For other people aging breaks the body down. Yet Jesus says, "Let not your heart be troubled"...or anxious, or stressed out, or worrisome. When we fully trust Jesus in our hearts his calm washes over us. Another verse says, "neither let it be afraid." Fear strikes the heart of all of us at various times when we experience uncomfortable stress. At those moments of severe stress we need to immediately ask God to give us his peace, hope, trust. He will give us a calming spirit, his Spirit of PEACE.

Chapter 35

"BELIEVE"—WITNESS THE MESSAGES OF TRUTH.

"Believe in God. He is invisible yet you believe in Him. Believe in Me- whom you have seen, witnessed My authority, My miracles, seen MY power at work, and have touched ME." —I John 1:1

It is still the simple fact that "...God so loved the world that He sent His only begotten Son, that whosoever believes in Him will not perish but have everlasting life." —John. 3:16.

L et's REPEAT WHAT POWER THEY SAW IN JESUS: let's examine each one of the proof texts.

THEY WITNESSED HIS WORDS: words are used hundreds of time to refer to the activity of speaking. In the Old Testament, "Then God spoke to Noah (his VOICE), (Gen. 21:1, 27. Ex. 6:10.12.) In speaking to the prophets: (Isa. 12, 24:3, 58:14; Jer. 1:1-12; 13:15).

God's people are encouraged to use their speech in such a way that reflects God's speech. Proverbs tells us "a word fitly spoken in like apples of gold in settings of silver."—Prov. 25:11

THEY WITNESSED HIS POWER: "All power and authority has been given to me by my Father in heaven"—Matthew 28:18 God is the source of all power. "Jesus sustains all things by the WORD of His power."(Hebrews 1:3) The assembled church possesses the power of the Lord Jesus. (I Corinthians 5:4). The Son of Man will come with "power and much glory." (Matthew 24:30; II Thessalonians. 1:7). Jesus ministers in the power of the Holy Spirit.(Luke 4:14) He has power over life, death, and the resurrection. He had power to lay his life down and the power to raise it up again.

THEY WITNESSED THE TRUE MEANING OF TRUTH: with his VOICE he speaks truth: "I AM the way, the truth and the life." His disciples were gathered together discussing their understanding about God and Jesus' relationship to the Father. To know God means that they also know Jesus Christ because he came from the Father. Jesus is God incarnate. Philip asked Jesus to show him the Father, and Jesus responds by saying he who has seen me has seen the Father also, for I and my Father are one. Jesus asks Philip whether he truly believes in him? "At least believe Me for the miracles you witnessed. You believe in God, believe also in Me."—John14:11 Intellectually we believe when we look at a watch that there is a designer; like the watch, there must be a watch-maker. This is a prime example of the cause and effect theory. A divine being must exist. These are imperative statements: "You believe in God–don't you?" Philip had to decide. The Bible says the devil believes and trembles knowing he is already defeated.

Belief in God is the admittance to his existence. Belief in Jesus Christ is to believe God sent his Son to redeem the world, bring salvation to all who will listen and trust his VOICE. "Now you must believe in Jesus Christ for there is no other name named among men whereby you can be saved. Are you listening Philip?"—John 14:9-11.

"Believe and you will be saved... You search the Scriptures, because you think that in them you have eternal life; and it is these that bear witness of Me; and you are unwilling to come to me, that you may have life."—John 5: 39.

In the gym I go to every day for my workout there is a man who used to walk with me. He was an alcoholic and eventually needed help so he attended three Alcohol Anonymous (AA) rehab meetings. In the AA program he said they had to believe in a Higher Being, though they never mentioned Jesus Christ because they don't promote any one religion. They just had to begin with a Higher Being who could help them. I admired him for going to this program. He was clean for many months. As we walked together over time I eventually encouraged him to study the Bible to see what else he needed to do, such as believing in God's Son. He said that was not necessary. I quoted several scriptures encouraging him otherwise but he rejected these. I see him at the gym every day but now he ignores me. I continue to pray for his salvation.

THEY WITNESSED HIS LIFE while here on earth. He called the Twelve Disciples to him and sent them out into the world as is witnesses. These were ordinary men coming from different walks of life. Peter, James and John, two fishermen and a tax collector. Jesus bound them together for one purpose only— to follow Christ. Jesus took their talents, anointed them and sent them out to become fishers of men. It was not only his words that made a lasting imprint on their lives it was the example of his life. When people view us doing they see our life as well as our words. Ask yourselves, 'Do we resonate with the character and command of Christ?' Christians are called upon by Jesus Christ to live the life of commitment and obedience to the Christ life. Don't worry about trying to be a verbal witness where people will not listen, live the life before them and love them to death. Perfect love casts out fear. Jesus said the greatest gift is the gift of love. Love is irresistible.

Matthew 28:18-20 is called the great commission. It applies to all believers and all churches today. "His VOICE speaks; all authority has been given to ME in heaven and on earth. Go therefore and make disciples of all nations, baptizing them in the name of the Father and the Son and the Holy Spirit. Teaching them to observe all that I commanded you' and lo, I AM with you always, even to the end of the age." Christians are his messengers until he returns for us. We have nothing to fear because we serve the One who has all power and authority. He has sent His Holy Spirit, this same Spirit that indwelt Jesus Christ, to be our comforter and guide. (John 14 thru 17 chapters). I Thessalonians 4:16: "For the Lord Himself will descend from heaven with a shout, with the VOICE of the archangel and with the trumpet of God, and the dead in Christ will rise first." WOW.

Christ has ALL authority. Nothing gets past his all seeing, all knowing eye. Along with all authority he has ALL POWER. The Greek word here means dynamite. It cannot do justice to his power. Now, if this is true, and the Bible says it is, then we Christians must leave all circumstances, events, world decisions, world leaders, in his hands. He is SOVEREIGN. We cannot change that statement. We can praise God for his promise. Therefore, we have nothing on this created earth to fear.

Chapter 36

THE ACTS OF THE APOSTLES

We are told that the Greek manuscript title is "Acts." The Greek word 'praxis' translates into 'Acts' as it was often used to describe the achievements/ acts of great men. The biblical Acts features notable figures of the church, the apostles, Stephen, Peter and Paul to name a few. The book could more accurately be called "The Acts of the Holy Spirit." (MacArthur)

THE WITNESS OF THE HOLY SPIRIT is seen throughout the book as the one empowering, strengthening being responsible for the growth of the early church following the day of Pentecost. It was written by Dr. Luke in 70 A.D. prior to the destruction of Jerusalem. The events that transpired in Acts reveal the work and ministry of the Holy Spirit during the first three decades of the church. Here we see the transformation of the Old Covenant to the New Covenant in the life of the church. We see how the church became immediately involved in persecution due to its witness Stephen We witness how the Holy Spirit filled his life. The apostles were busy preaching and teaching the word. There were widows and others who needed someone to care for their needs. (Acts 6) The apostles said to set apart someone who was of good character and repute, full of the Holy Spirit and wisdom, which can do this work. They selected Stephen and six other men. After prayer the apostles laid their hands on them. (Acts 6:5,6). As a result the ministry continued to prosper and multiplied greatly.

Stephen full of grace and divine power was working great wonders. The Holy Spirit confounded all who heard him. There were those who detested what he was doing and set out to accuse him falsely. So he was taken before the High Priest and questioned. Stephen gives his powerful message relating the whole history of God's Word beginning with their father Abraham. The Jews were cut to the quick and grabbed Stephen, took him outside the city and stoned him to death. Stephen filled with the Holy Spirit prayed, looking up into heaven, asked the Lord to accept his spirit and died. He asked the Lord to forgive them for what they did to him. And they laid his garments at a young man's feet- Saul. (Acts 6;7) Stephen is a great example of a witness to the power of God and the Holy Spirit in a time of crises. He was full of grace and divine power.

Peter (petra- the rock) is an interesting person because he was the fisherman who was transformed by Jesus. He was bold, brash at times, but loyal to the teeth. Yet when Christ was captured by the priest's guards and taken before the High Priest, Caiaiphas, Peter denied he believed in Jesus three times. Jesus told him earlier he would do this and Peter, the rock, said "No way will I deny you Lord." Would we deny Jesus to save our own skin? Jesus said in the last days many will deny they knew him and walk away.

Two times people in the courtyard and at the gate recognized Peter as being with Jesus but Peter denied no connection to Jesus with an oath. Three times he denied Jesus was his friend and in the distance a rooster crowed. Peter remembered Jesus' words and wept. Later Jesus forgave Peter for denying him three times. He called Peter the rock (Gk.petros- a small stone), and on this rock (petra; a foundation builder) Jesus was the real foundation builder, not Peter. Jesus would build his assembly (ekkilasian).(Matthew16:18). This is a play on words. Peter is the *little stone* while Jesus Christ is a *boulder*.

The church is built on the "Living Stone." Jesus Christ is the "Chief Cornerstone" of the church. (I Peter 2:5). Scholar John MacArthur states that in Matthew Christ calls it 'My Church' emphasizing that he alone is its "Architect, Builder, Owner and Lord. And the gates of hell shall not prevail against it." Because of Peter's commitment and faith he would suffer many things for Jesus and ultimately paid with his life, hanging upside down on a cross. Judas betrayed Jesus for thirty pieces of silver and later went out and hanged himself. Peter later repented, was forgiven by Jesus and was sent out to preach the Gospel to the world. Judas committed suicide.

THE DISCIPLES WITNESSED HIS RESURRECTION. The women were the first to go to Jesus' tomb. They found the huge stone rolled away from the entrance and Jesus was not there. The angel of the Lord spoke to them: "He is risen, He is not dead." (Mark 16:6,7; Matthew 28:5,6 C.S) We have the witness of his resurrection in our minds and hearts, because he lives, we will live also with him. When a person gives himself the time to read the full story about Jesus Christ, listening to his VOICE, he will realize the truth contained in the Scriptures. Man could not have faked the truth. Christianity should have died at Jesus' death on the cross. Over 500 people witnessed seeing Jesus Christ following his resurrection. He had a meal with his disciples. (I Corinthians 15:3-6). Paul warns us: "If Christ has not risen, and then our preaching is in vain, your faith is in vain."—I Corinthians 15:14

Jesus Christ speaks his Words in his VOICE with the same power and authority as the Father—" I and my Father are One." In Colossians Paul speaks of the power and authority that is in Jesus Christ. "He is the image of the invisible God, the firstborn of all creation. For by him all things were created in heaven and on earth, visible and invisible, whether thrones or dominions or rulers or authorities- all things were created through him and for him. He is before all things, and in him all things hold together. He is the head of the body, the church…for in him all the fullness of God was pleased to dwell, and through him to reconcile to himself all things whether on earth or in heaven, making peace by the blood of his cross."—Col. 1: 5-20 When Jesus Christ speaks his Words and the people listen to his VOICE, lives are changed forever.

Paul delivered these words to the Colossian church showing the power and presence of Christ. He spoke what he knew from his personal experience. As a Pharisee he was a persecutor of the church. When he met Christ on the road to Damascus he was transformed, saved to follow Christ the rest of his life. The unbelievable transformation of Paul's life from a persecutor of the church to becoming a pro-claimer and protector in his conversion and commitment to follow Jesus Christ should cause us to consider what our own response should be to Jesus Christ. Paul's transformation from Judaism to Christ was miraculous.

Again, I return to the transformation of the German theologian Dietrich Bonhoeffer. When he graduated from the University of Berlin, where he completed his doctoral work at the age of 21, he began preaching and teaching the Bible. BUT, at this time he was still not a Christian. From the powerful book *Bonhoeffer Study Guide: The Life and Writings of Dietrich Bonhoeffer* by Eric Metaxis is a letter written to his Bonhoeffer's girlfriend describing his spiritual transformation (most scholars believed to be in 1931): "...For the first time I discovered the Bible...I had not yet become a Christian. It became clear to me that the life of a servant of Jesus Christ must belong to the Church. The Sermon of the Mount did it, before I was quite pleased with myself." The Holy Spirit came into his life.

In his day Martin Luther had a similar experience to Bonhoeffer's. Luther was a Roman Catholic. One time he was on his way home when lightening struck right in front of him. This experience led him to become a monk, and doing everything he could to be rid of his sins. He still felt burdened. He taught the Psalms and Romans at the University of Wittenberg. During this time Romans 1:17 hit him again and again: "For in it is the righteousness of God is revealed from faith to faith: as it is written, But the righteous man shall live by faith,"... "the just shall live by faith, and this faith is in the Son of

God alone, not by works of righteousness which he had done." The Holy Spirit set Luther on fire for God and the Reformation is history.

Another testament to the transformative power of accepting Christ is how C.S. Lewis, the great Oxford scholar, started out as an atheist and later became a Christian. In his autobiography of his reluctant conversion, he described himself as the "prodigal who is brought kicking, struggling, resentful, and darting his eyes in every direction for a chance of escape…" Lewis didn't find God, God found him. On Divine mercy he wrote," The hardness of God is kinder than the softness of men, and His compulsion is our liberation." The Holy Spirit opened his eyes to God's truth. He had a strong commitment to truth and his writings show it. "Truth is discovered when thought conforms to reality. Honesty is crucial." This he made clear in his writings *Surprised By Joy: The Shape of My Early Life* "The universe rings true wherever you fairly test it." Lewis was unashamed of his Christian frame of reference; from the time of his conversion, it was the integrating force behind his thought, life and writing. He wrote, "I believe in Christianity as I believe the sun is risen not only because I see it but because by it I see everything else."

This quote is from *The Quotable Lewis*, authors Wayne Martindale and Jerry Root.

JESUS IS THE LANGUAGE OF GOD
He is God's representative en fleshed.
"I and my Father are One,"
Jesus is God.

God speaks to us, we hear his VOICE in his son Jesus Christ and the Holy Spirit. Listen to the Apostles Creed: *I believe in God the Father almighty, maker of heaven and earth and in Jesus Christ, His Son our Lord: who was conceived by the Holy Spirit, born of the Virgin Mary, suffered under Pontius Pilate, was crucified, dead and buried. He descended into Hades; the third day He rose again from the dead: He ascended into heaven, and sits on the right hand of God, the Father Almighty; from thence He shall come to judge the quick and the dead. I believe in the Holy Spirit, the holy Christian Church, communion of saints, the forgiveness of sins, the resurrection of the body, and the life everlasting. Amen*

The early church began to grow and spread outward as people became Christians to other towns and cities. They followed Christ's words to take the Gospel to the nations and people baptizing them in the name of the Father, the Son and the Holy Spirit. In the first century there were homes (house churches) where people gathered together for prayer, worship, teaching, sing songs and have communion. What a fellowship, what a joy divine. Churches were born in Palestine, Antioch, Damascus, Corinth and Ephesus to name a few. The first followers were of Jewish descent and following Pentecost the Gospel spread to the Gentiles as recorded in the book of Acts. Paul founded many Gentile- Christian congregations. God cut Paul out especially to minister to the Gentiles. Listen to his witness in Ephesians 3:1-7. It was a mystery at first how the Gentiles would be saved. It was revealed by the Holy Spirit that took over Paul's life: "This mystery, it is this, that the Gentiles are now to be fellow heirs (with the Jews), members of the same body, and joint partakers (sharing) in the same divine promise in Christ through their acceptance of the glad tidings (the good news) of the Gospel."

Out of these first beginnings came the confessions of faith that eventually developed into what we know as The Apostles Creed today. This confession became a part of the spiritual ministry of the church and was included as a part of the worship services. Different creeds were formed to combat all types of false teachings and heresies being bandied about that ran contrary to the truth in God's Word. False teachers were trying to infiltrate the church. The different creeds are often found in the hymnbooks used for worship. Ephesians 5:19, 20: "Speak out to one another in psalms and hymns and spiritual songs, offering praise with voices and instruments, making melody with all your hearts to the LORD. AT ALL TIMES AND FOR EVERYTHING GIVING THANKS in the name of the Lord Jesus Christ to God the Father." The Holy Spirit is sent by the Son and the Father to fulfill his ministry. He has the same power and authority. When was the last time you gave thanks to God for your life, good health, for food on the table?

In the New Testament Gospel of Luke (the book that is full of surprises) the angel appeared to Zachariah, the priest, as he was performing his duties in the Temple. "You are going to have a child." He had prayed for his wife Elizabeth who was barren and advanced in years. In those days to be married and yet barren was a sign something was wrong. The angel Gabriel told him they heard his prayers and that his wife will bear a son and you must call him John (meaning God is favorable). He became John the Baptist the precursor of Jesus Christ. (Luke1: 11-20)

What is the purpose of God blessing Elizabeth and Zachariah?

- First, she was going to have a child.
- Second, this child will have a special name, John.
- Third, he will be filled with the Holy Spirit before he is born.
- Fourth, he will turn back many sons of Israel to God.
- Fifth, he will be the forerunner of Jesus Christ, preparing the people to receive him when he arrives.
- Sixth, many will rejoice at his birth.

Zachariah is speechless. "How can this be, how can I know for certain? For I am an old man and my wife is advanced in years." Gabriel was sent personally by God to speak to Zachariah. "You shall be silent (speechless) until the day this takes place. Why? It is because you did not believe my words… You refused to listen to My VOICE." What is it about this story that sounds so familiar? Return to the Old Testament and the story of Abraham and his barren wife. Both stories show the consequences of not believing God's promise. When God makes a promise he keeps it!

Can the finite mind comprehend these marvelous events that the Scriptures declare as truth? No, because we are damaged goods. We are not whole. We cannot save ourselves. We need the witness of the Holy Spirit to speak to us, to fill our lives to the fullest with God's love. This is God's divine revelation on how all these events happened "for us." You have to resolve in your own mind that God knew what he was doing all along throughout history. God's rule is orderly and not chaotic. He knows the beginning and the end of life. God said: (his VOICE) "I AM Alpha and Omega, the first and the last."

Chapter 37

GOD'S DIVINE REVELATION...
THE MYSTERY IS SOLVED

M y students: can you leave your queries behind for a moment and grasp what is being said here? This is God's divine revelation to his intervening power to plant the seed in a woman's body to bring forth the humanized Son of God to bring salvation to the whole world. God did what no man could do by himself. Do you think you are capable to question the manuscript God gave us in his divine revelation? Only a fool would try it. As the ancient Egyptian would say, "...thus shall it be written and thus shall it be done." The finality of it is certain; nothing can change it. It's imperative. This is God's VOICE.

When you study the life of Christ you see why he had to come to take our place and die. God makes no mistakes. He rules with power and authority. All he asks us to do is believe and you will be saved. In Luke 4:16-21, Jesus delivered a very powerful message when he entered the synagogue on the Sabbath and stood up to read. The scroll of the prophet Isaiah was handed to him. He unrolled it and found the place where it was written,

All those who were present heard His VOICE;
The Spirit of the Lord is upon Me, (this is the Holy
Spirit), because
He anointed Me- to preach the Gospel to the poor.
He has sent Me to
Proclaim release of the captives, and recovery of
sight to the blind, to set free those who are down-
trodden, to proclaim the favorable year   o f
the Lord. (Isaiah 61:1-3, Lev. 25:10)

He rolled up the scroll gave it to the attendant and sat down; and the eyes of all in the synagogue were fixed upon him. And he said to them: "Today this Scripture has been fulfilled in your hearing."—Luke 4:21

Note what Jesus said: "The Spirit of the Lord is upon me." (This is his anointing from God). The Holy Spirit descended from heaven and rested on him at his baptism by John the Baptist. Then a VOICE FROM HEAVEN spoke through the cloud: "This is my beloved Son, in whom I AM well pleased." This is Messianic. Christ is the one Isaiah is talking about. He is called to preach the Gospel to the poor. He is sent to set captives free; all who are bound by and death. To recover sight to the blind (to those living in the darkness Jesus brings light and new life) in the favorable "Year of the Lord." (Luke 4:16-21. John 3:16)

This is a direct quote from Isaiah 53:1-3. This is a picture of the suffering servant Jesus Christ: this is the Messianic section of Old Testament:

Who has believed our message and to whom has the arm of the Lord been revealed? He grew up before him like a tender shoot, and like a root out of dry ground.

He had no beauty or majesty to attract us to him, nothing in his appearance that we should desire him.

He was despised and rejected by men, a man of sorrows, and familiar with suffering. Like one from whom men hide their faces, he was despised and we esteemed him not.

We all like sheep have gone stray, each of us have turned to his own way; and the Lord has laid on him the iniquity of us all.

This is God's perfect timing for the Gospel to be delivered to the world. Isaiah's prophecy was given almost 700 years before the birth of Jesus Christ. It is ongoing and not finished until the last soul is saved then the end will come. At first the Jews in attendance were pleased at his Words but as they pondered over them they became enraged and wanted to kill Jesus because he who was a lowly carpenter's son blasphemed God in making himself equal with God. (Luke 4:28-30)

In this prophecy from Isaiah we have a confirmation that the Old and New Testament are indeed valid and reliable. It is the fulfillment of the Old Testament. Jesus himself refers to the writers and prophets of the Old Testament throughout his teaching ministry. In Luke 24:25ff, following his resurrection he spoke (his VOICE), to those who were present: "O foolish men and slow of heart to BELIEVE in all that the prophets have spoken." Matt. 26:24: "Was it not necessary for Christ to suffer those things and to enter into His glory?" And beginning with Moses and with all the prophets, he explained to them the things concerning himself in all the Scriptures." These verses validate each other. WHAT A Bible lesson they received from Jesus. Later they ask Jesus to join with them for mealtime and he did: "And Jesus took the bread and broke it and gave it to them, and immediately their eyes were opened."—Matthew 24:29-32. Wow! Then the Holy Spirit confirmed his words (his VOICE) to them. What a glorious awakening.

Here is the key phrase: "O FOOLISH MEN SLOW TO HEART TO BELIEVE." To God our eyes would be opened to receive his words and to believe. Everything that Jesus Christ says is backed-up by the Father who sent Him: "I and my Father are One, I can do nothing except what the Father tells Me." (John 14,15,16,17). Who are these 'Foolish men'? They represent all those who have, in one way or another, heard the VOICE of God spoken through his Word who stubbornly reject the truth, i.e., agnostic, atheists, doubters and liars.

The Gospel of Mark goes right to the heart of the message telling us that John the Baptist was in the wilderness preaching a baptism of repentance for the forgiveness of sins. God sent him forth to prepare the way for the Lord's appearance. Many people followed John out of Judea and Jerusalem and were baptized by him. He declared: "… after me One is coming mightier than I, and I am not fit to stoop down and untie the thong of His sandals. I baptize you with water; but He will baptize you with the Holy Spirit."—Mark 1:1-8

Jesus Christ is anointed by the appearance of the dove (symbol of love). This is an epic moment for John the

Baptist. He was the precursor of Christ. In Mark 1:9 we read: "...and it came about in those days that Jesus came from Nazareth in Galilee, and was baptized by John. And immediately coming up out of the water, He saw the heavens opening, and the Spirit like a dove descending upon Him, and A VOICE OUT OF HEAVEN; you are My beloved Son, in you I AM well pleased." This is God's VOICE.

Dr. A.B. Simpson wrote extensively about the importance of the Holy Spirit. He writes about the figure of the dove as the suggestive icon of peace. The dove that flew out from Noah's Ark was the messenger of peace, and brought back an olive branch as a symbol of reconciliation. Thus is the Holy Spirit the messenger of peace with God through the Lord Jesus Christ. He leads the soul to understand and accept the message of grace and mercy and to find peace with God which keeps the heart and mind in Jesus Christ. Wherever the Holy Spirit reigns there is peace.

Opposite of the peaceful dove is the black raven. Edgar Allen Poe's poem The Raven describes the restless nature of the dark bird— *"Ghastly grim and ancient raven wandering from the nightly shore...Quoth the raven, 'Nevermore.'* Restlessly passing to and fro, to and fro, to and fro a troubled spirit of evil. It finds no quiet or contentment even in the pleasures of sin. The raven is driven from excitement to excitement. Without Christ, people's lives are like the raven's—restless, unsettled and forlorn. There is no peace in the heart; there is only the vain pursuit of rest, until at last it is thrown upon the wild billows of a lost eternity, the victim of everlasting disquietude...nevermore.

The dove is a symbol of purity, harmony, peace and rest. *Harmless as a dove* is Christ's interpretation of the beautiful emblem. The Spirit of God, which is purity itself, cannot dwell in an unclean heart. The dove is the symbol of gentleness. The Comforter is gentle, tender, and full of patience and love. The heart in which the Holy Spirit dwells will always be characterized by gentleness, quietness, meekness and forbearance. The Holy Spirit is the Spirit of love. (I Corinthians 13) This is the Spirit that Christ seeks to dwell in us; the Spirit of meekness and obedience to his will.

Whenever you see the reference to the 'Son' or the 'Father' it is capitalized because we are speaking of divinity. Jesus subordinated himself to the Father's will. The English Dictionary defines *subordinate* as inferior to be placed below in rank, power, in importance or under the power and authority of another, subservient or submissive. The latter definition can refer to Jesus Christ.

What is the meaning of obedience?

Jesus Christ was obedient to the Father's will. He subordinated himself to fulfill the righteous requirements of the law and obedience to God the Father. When he subordinated his will to the Father's will it did not mean that Jesus was somehow less than God. He possesses all the divine attributes and excellencies of the Trinity. "He is coequal, consubstantiation, and co-eternal with the Father."—John 10:30; 14:9 In the incarnation Christ surrendered only the prerogatives of deity but nothing of the divine essence. At the same time Jesus accepted all the essential characteristics of humanity when he became man. (Phil. 2:5-8, Col. 2:9)

PART II

THE LIFE OF THE CHRISTIAN WHO IS LED BY THE HOLY SPIRIT

Chapter 38

IS THE HOLY SPIRIT NECESSARY?

The Holy Spirit is sent to fulfill the ministry of the Trinity bringing us to repentance and redemption by our faith in Jesus. I know people have difficulty understanding the ministry of the Holy Spirit. Let me explain: the Trinity consists of God the Father, God the Son and God the Holy Spirit. God' s work involved the creation of the universe, including all the galaxies and planets. He created all life forms, water, plants, animals, fish in the seas, birds in the sky. In mother earth he formed man of the dust of the ground and breathed into his nostrils the breath of life, and man became a living soul. Animals do not have a soul nor the ability to reason and communicate with man. Man was a spiritual being until the fall. After the fall he lost his spiritual connection with God. In his fallen nature he could no longer have a relationship with God. He was dead in trespasses and sin. As a lost soul he could not rectify his situation in his own power.

This is why God sent his only begotten Son into the world. Only Jesus Christ could satisfy God by taking on the sins of the world and dying on a cross for sin. Now all who are born again through faith in Christ can have fellowship with the Father. This is what Jesus was tying to tell Nicodemus: "You must be born again. Then you receive the Holy Spirit into your life. You are a new creature, a new creation. The Holy Spirit lives in our bodies and he reveals whatever Jesus Christ tells him to do. You can't see him but you can hear him in the wind or in the breath of God. Before Jesus left his disciples to return to the Father in heaven he told them to wait for the promise of the Holy Spirit."—Acts 1:1-8

Following His resurrection Jesus presented himself to his disciples.

He told them to stay put in Jerusalem and wait. As one writer put it, if someone who was just raised from the dead told you to wait I am sure you would obey. The Father had promised that John the Baptist will baptize with water, BUT you shall be baptized with the Holy Spirit in just a few days. But you shall receive POWER when the Holy Spirit has come upon you and you shall be my witnesses (My VOICE) both in Jerusalem, in Judea, in Samaria and to the whole world.

Why was it important for them to wait? What was the result? They received power from on high. Can the Christian or the church accomplish anything without the Holy Spirit? They can and do try to duplicate his work in the flesh, but to no avail. Can we as individuals accomplish anything for Christ without the Holy Spirit? No. "Not by works of righteousness lest any man should boast…salvation is a Free Gift From GOD for all who will believe by faith."—John 3:16. On the day the Pentecost arrives. (Acts 2:1f) (denoting the descent of the Holy Spirit).The biblical scholar F.F. Bruce calls this

"The beginning of a new age," meaning, of course, the sending of the Holy Spirit.

"And suddenly there came from heaven a noise like a violent, rushing wind, and it filled the whole house where they were sitting... And they were all filled with the Holy Spirit."—Acts 2:2 What happened? Was this necessary? Was it important to obey Jesus Christ? The Holy Spirit is sent by the Father and the Son as a witness and to fill every believer's heart. Do you see the importance of the Holy Spirit? Is he a person? The Holy Spirit is God's voice. Does he have personality? Yes, again. "As a result the place here was set on fire with the presence and power of the Holy Spirit." (Acts 2:1ff.) Different languages were spoken for those who needed it. The place shook with the wind of God.

The Bible tells us of various means God uses to get peoples attention; the Holy Spirit is involved in the Old Testament period; at creation. In Genesis 1:1 the Bible says: "...and the Spirit of God was moving over the surface of the waters." Wherever you find God working you know the Holy Spirit is not far behind doing his part. Moses led the Israelites out of Egypt and the Red sea split in two and gave dry land for the people to cross. In the wilderness God gave them manna from heaven and water in the dry desert.

The disciples were ordinary men who needed extraordinary power. This power had to come from Jesus Christ, the same power he received at his baptism. He fulfilled the Father's will to transfer the powerful message of good news to His disciples. But, the disciples needed the Holy Spirit that indwelt Jesus. Pentecost changed the course of the good news. It would spread to Judea,

Samaria, to the Roman world and beyond. Two thousand plus years later we are the beneficiaries of their work. Praise the Lord.

Dr. R. C. Sproul, president of Reformation Bible College and co-pastor of Saint Andrew's Chapel in Sanford, Florida is author of *Scripture Alone* and *Can I Trust the Bible?* In his commentary of Acts he points out "no one has ever been saved by somebody else's faith. We all belong to groups. We are part of a family, or a school class, or a football team. We are all part of a community, a state and a nation. We have memberships in a host of corporate, private and public organizations. But, in the final analysis, when we stand before God we stand or fall on the basis of our faith in Christ or our lack of it. In that sense, redemption is personal and individual." We stand alone before God.

The Holy Spirit can be grieved: Eph. 4:30: "and grieve not the Holy Spirit of God, whereby (because of), you are sealed unto the day of redemption" What does that mean? The Holy Spirit is grieved when God's children refuse to change their old habits of sin for a new life and the righteousness of God. Such responses by the Holy Spirit indicate he is a person. Personal pronouns are also used to reveal his personhood. He is called the Spirit of truth. The Spirit will not always strive with man.

Parents are grieved when they see their children behaving in direct disobedience to their wishes. There is a whole lot that goes on when marriages dissolve and the family is split up. Children often bear the brunt of such willful disobedience of parents in their vows to each other and to God. Dire consequences follow. Similarly, Christians grieve the Holy Spirit when they refuse to give up their old life style in obedience to Christ and the Word. In I Corinthians 2:11: "For what man knows the things of man, save the spirit of man which is in him, even so the things of God knows no man, but the Spirit of God." Here the Holy Spirit is interceding, guiding and glorifying Christ. It is his VOICE speaking. Oh what power…dynamite power.

The Holy Spirit intercedes on behalf of the saints. "For all who are being led by the Spirit of God, these are the sons of God."—Romans 8:14. And Vs. 26: "In the same way the Spirit helps our weaknesses; for we do not know how to pray as we should, but the Spirit Himself intercedes for us with groaning too deep for words." The believer groans for the restoration of God's kingdom and the resurrection of the body. The earth also groans from the day Adam and Eve brought a curse on themselves when they fell out with God. Because we are weak and born in sin we need help even when we pray. The disciples asked the Lord to teach us to pray and here is where the Lord's Prayer came. There are times when we are at a loss of just how to pray and what to pray for. This is where we can ask the Holy Spirit to intercede for us. We ultimately conclude our prayer with "Thy will be done." Our will and God's will are often in conflict because we want things. In Shakespeare's Hamlet, I believe it was King Richard who in desperation, went to his room to pray—"My words fly up, my thoughts remain below. Words without thoughts never to heaven go." Hamlet found him out.

The Holy Spirit can be blasphemed. And we have the warning against blaspheming the Holy Spirit. What does that mean? Mathew 12:31, 32: "Wherefore I say unto you, All manner of sin and blasphemy shall be forgiven unto men: but blasphemy against the Holy Spirit shall not be forgiven unto men. And whosoever speaks a word against the Son of Man, it shall be forgiven him; but whosoever speaks against the Holy Spirit, it shall not be forgiven him, neither in this world, neither in the world to come." The Jews accused Jesus of blaspheming when he forgave sins and assumed messianic rights that they regarded as belonging to God alone.

The Pharisees deliberately rejected the signs and miraculous deeds Jesus performed before their eyes. They attributed the signs to the work of the devil. Look at the woes Jesus pronounced against the scribes, Pharisees and the cities that rejected him. (Mathew 23:13-36) They refused to acknowledge that Jesus was God. Jesus states that people who reject him at first because of ignorance can be forgiven for speaking against him (even swearing my dad, a blue collar worker, did this all the time), or for persecuting his prophets, as Paul did while he was a Pharisee. When they have heard the Gospel and reject the Word it is another story. They rejected the Holy Spirit, who came to witness and declare Jesus Christ. You can read more about this in John MacArthur's *Bible Commentary* on Matthew 12:31-32.

Chapter 39

THE LIFE OF THE CHRISTIAN LED BY THE HOLY SPIRIT

J esus Christ laid aside his divine prerogatives of deity with the Father, left his place with the Father, took our place and became the servant among Men. (Phil, 2:5-8) He never divested himself of any of the essential attributes of deity. This same truth is applied to the Holy Spirit. Jesus Christ sent the Holy Spirit in full harmony with the Father. The Spirit of Truth, the Comforter, the Advocate is sent to be with us forever. Jesus promised the disciples that when the Holy Spirit comes upon you, you would *receive power*. The Person and work of the Holy Spirit is profoundly important to the born again Christian. He prays daily for guidance and the anointing of the Holy Spirit.

It has been my experience that Jesus' ministry is vital to the Church today. Jesus told his disciples just before he departed to be with the Father: "I will send the Comforter (Gk. Paraclatos) and He will teach you everything I have said unto you, And He will bring these things to your remembrance."—John 14:26

Bonhoeffer states that without Jesus Christ the church does not exist. The same can be said about the Holy Spirit. One may find many churches that carry-on without Christ's presence, They may be mega churches filled with people who look for messages that give them personal gratification, cheap grace without the cross. The Lord gives them over to believe their lies. (Romans 1:18f) In other words, let them believe in their false philosophies and their unbelief in God's warnings. Let them die in their sins and await the judgment of God.

Part Two discusses how important it is for Christians to understand the work and ministry of the Holy Spirit. For several years I have been studying the scriptures and reading definitive and exhaustive books on the importance of this subject. Why? Because I sense many Christians, including myself have been missing out on the blessings and promises Christ gives us with through the Holy Spirit's work. We have orphaned ourselves with immature ideas and excuses about the Holy Spirit. Webster's dictionary (11th edition) has several definitions for the word 'orphan.' The one I like best says: "… to be deprived of some protection or advantage." How can we apply this to what the Scriptures tell us concerning the Holy Spirit?

First, let's consider these important questions:

How do you view the Holy Spirit? Is the Holy Spirit a real person or is he an 'IT' in your mind? Is the Holy Spirit someone or something tangible you can rely on?

Before you can understand the Holy Spirit you must acknowledge His existence as the third Person of the

Trinity. Ephesians 3:16: "Paul's prayer, that Christ would grant you, according to the riches of His glory, to be strengthened with power through His Spirit in the inner man..."

Do you worship him the same as you worship the Father and the Son, Jesus Christ? If he is a divine person is the Holy Spirit worthy of our praise, worship, adoration, honor, devotion of our faith, our love and our full attention?

Romans 5:5: "Hope does not disappoint, because the love of God has been poured out within our hearts through the Holy Spirit who was given to us."

Do you know and understand the Holy Spirit has claim on your life? For a lot of people this is difficult because they don't want to believe the Holy Spirit seeks our full surrender and obedience to his will, just as God required when he sent his only begotten Son, Jesus Christ to die on the cross for our salvation (John 3:16).

"Jesus sent His Spirit, the same Spirit that indwelt Him here on earth and became humanized in Jesus."— John 14:18-21; Galatians 3:13-14

If you are a Christian how much do you think you can accomplish in own strength without the Holy Spirit?

John 15:4: "Abide in Me, and I in you. As the branch cannot bear fruit of itself, unless it abides in the vine, so neither can you, unless you abide in Me."

II Corinthians 3:17: "Now the Lord is the Spirit, and where the Spirit of the Lord is, there is freedom." Jesus made it clear that "without Me you can do nothing."

Our problem is we want to live our lives on our own terms leaving God out. According to the Bible no one can say he is truly a Christian and still deny the Holy Spirit access to his life. Jesus said, "If you love me, keep my commandments." Paul said, follow me even as I follow Christ. To believe is to obey. We can't have it both ways, a double minded man is unstable in all his actions. This means ALL our works, every single thing we try to do in our own strength, accomplishes nothing in God's sight as his righteousness is concerned. Whatsoever you do, do all to the glory of God. Once we are saved and we trust wholly in Jesus Christ whatever we do it is in his name and for his glory

In the New Testament, how does God make Himself known today?

Jesus Christ is seated at the right hand of the Father. The answer is in what Jesus promised his disciples before he departed into heaven. In the Gospel of John chapter 14 we read: "And I will ask the Father, and He will give you another Helper, and He will be with you forever." (Vs.16).

In the New Testament the word of God centers on Jesus Christ and the Holy Spirit. Here we will discover how the Holy Spirit is used by Jesus Christ to carry on His work. This is a crucial section in the life of every believer

A Hymn: Spirit of the living God, fall afresh on me,
Spirit of the living God, fall afresh on me,
Melt me, mold me, fill me, use me.
Spirit of the living God, fall afresh on me.
May this be your prayer.

Chapter 40

HOW TO KNOW THE HOLY SPIRIT PERSONALLY

E veryone needs The Holy Spirit in his/her life. Everyone. Dr. R.C. Sproul reminds us: "We are to be people of the Holy Spirit, as well as of the Son and the Father." There are those who shy away from discussing the Holy Spirit because they think he is a mysterious wonder or a power to be left alone. Some people believe that in order to receive the Holy Spirit they must have an out of body experience. This is a misinterpretation of the scriptures. The question we need to ask ourselves is how can I get to know the Holy Spirit personally?

Dr. John Walvoord, theologian, educator, author and long-time president of the Dallas Theological Seminary writes, "The personality of the Holy Spirit has been subjected to denial and neglect through the centuries of the Christian church and is seldom understood by twentieth century Christians. Many people do not understand the Person and work of the Holy Spirit because they have never experienced His presence and power in their lives.

For some people it is a subject they would like to leave alone. Perhaps they are afraid of what will happen to them if they allow the Holy Spirit to work in their lives. They may have to give up something they want to keep. There are those (Pentecostal), who believe that when you receive the Holy Spirit you should speak in tongues. As a result many false teachings and doctrines have scared people away from seeking the Holy Spirit's power in their lives."

Through continued study of the Holy Spirit through Bible teachings we will dispel unwarranted fears. I refer to several authors who have studied the scriptures extensively regarding this very important third person of the Godhead. These books enlighten us to the role of the Holy Spirit in a Christian's life—Dr. R.A. Torrey's book, *The Presence and Work of the Holy Spirit*, has been reprinted several times. Diedrick Bonhoeffer's *The cost of Discipleship*, is a classic required reading in many seminaries. Dr. Jack Deere's, *Surprised by the Power of the Spirit: Discovering how God Speaks and Heals Today* and Dr. William D. Mounce's *Expository Dictionary of Old and New Testament Words* are excellent scholarship focus on the Holy Spirit.

This message is only for the person who is interested in Jesus Christ—If you are a Christian the Holy Spirit is already at work in your life. The non-believer will not understand what we are talking about UNTIL they receive Christ. The Bible says: "God is spirit, and those who worship Him must worship in spirit and truth."— John 4:24 "As many as are led by the spirit of God they are the sons of God."—Romans 8:14 You will notice I have repeated some scriptures several times. This is to fix them firmly in our minds so God can speak to us. We must be much in prayer and ask the Holy Spirit to minister to you.

In a recent class I taught for Buffalo Bible Institute on the person and work of the Holy Spirit, I asked these crucial questions:

- Do you believe the Bible is the inspired word of God from his word through the ministry of the Holy Spirit?
- Do you believe in the Trinity? That the Trinity is God The Father, God the Son and God the Holy Spirit and they are One in unity, co-equal, co-existent and co-eternal?
- Do you believe in God's claim on your life once you are born the second time — the new birth?
- Do you believe the Holy Spirit is sent to bear witness to us? That we are saved, and then to be our comforter and guide through life?
- Does the Holy Spirit have claim on your life?

Begin by setting aside all preconceived notions, ideas and biases you have held regarding the Holy Spirit and the reason why you believe and do certain things. The Bible says: "The heart is deceitful and desperately wicked. Who can understand it? The false spirit is against God's truths and he will try to deceive you."—Jeremiah 17:9 We may hold some ideas and thoughts that have nothing to do with Scripture. We just picked them up along the way. Begin by asking God to cleanse our hearts and minds and help us to be open to what he would teach us from his word. In our study of the Holy Spirit we want to deal with certainties not opinions or conjecture.

I just finished reading Dr. Jack Deere's *Surprised by the Power of the Spirit: Discovering how God Speaks and Heals Today* and I want to share his thoughts to begin a quest for the truth about the Holy Spirit. Deere is a Doctor of Theology, a professor in Dallas Theological Seminary and a pastor of a church. He has called himself a dispensationalist (believes the work of healing, and miracles ceased at Pentecost). It is like saying the Holy Spirit was no longer ministering in the Church or the lives of believers. He found out otherwise. Deere's personal experience gives insight into how God can change preset ideas and belief suppositions. By accepting Jesus Christ I mean they have listened to the Word (God's message, his VOICE) and they have been convicted a sinner and convinced that Jesus Christ is God's Son who came to save them, and they have confessed their sin and a need for forgiveness. Romans 10:9-10 is their prayer of confession. With the mouth confession is made that tells others of your decision to live for Jesus. At that moment of confession the Holy Spirit enters the heart and the recipient becomes a new creation in Christ Jesus.

The next step in building a relationship with the Holy Spirit is to allow God's VOICE to fill your heart and mind with his Word. People are like empty vessels that need to be filled with God's Word. A baby needs food and nourishment, which is the Word of God. II Timothy 3:15-16: "God's word must become alive, a fire in our souls. You need to spend time in study and prayer to allow the Holy Spirit to teach you God's word. You are a new creation in Christ Jesus." Study, and study and absorb God's Word, soak it up. "Walk in the spirit and you will not fulfill the lusts of the flesh."—Galatians 5:16.

We are God's walking, talking witnesses. People always say there are two things we don't want to talk about in polite company—politics and religion. It sounds like the devil is in the mix. When relatives get together we clam up. But as born again Christians who believe in Jesus Christ we should use every opportunity to declare his Word. Jesus sends us out as 'the light of the world;' as 'salt of the earth.' We should wait for doors of opportunity to open and then give our personal life story of how God met us. Did Jesus stop speaking for the Father before Pilate? Did the Apostles keep silent when faced with persecution and suffering? They spoke the Word of God with more boldness and power of the Holy Spirit. There is an awareness and sensitivity of God's work in your life, cleansing, purifying and molding you into his vessel. You need to give up old habits and replace them with God's will for your life.

You are being led by the Holy Spirit to surrender everything to God, body, soul and spirit. "If a man loves me he will keep my commandments. Walk not after the flesh but after the spirit." ...therefore know no condemnation to those who are in Christ Jesus. For the law of the Spirit of the life in Christ Jesus has set you free from the law of sin and death."—Romans 8:1 Jesus is the potter, we are the clay. Here is a clear example Paul gives regarding the Spirit and the flesh. Where are you in your spiritual journey? After much speculation confusion and doubt we reach a point in our spiritual journey where we ask Jesus to be the LORD of our life. You have willingly denied yourself and are willing to take up your cross and are determined to follow Jesus.

Each person may come to this life's conclusion via a little different route but the Bible makes it clear it has to happen if one is to follow Jesus Christ all the way. Jesus said that if you love me you will keep my commandments, take up your cross and follow me. Dietrich Bonhoeffer put it like this: "…when Christ calls a man he must deny himself daily. Christ calls us to come and die…"(completely to self)…"The cross is laid on every Christian."

When Christ calls us to follow him it is the call to abandon ALL the attachments to this world. It is the dying of the old man. As we embark on discipleship, we surrender ourselves in union with his death (His Cost of discipleship). When Jesus called his disciples they had to leave home to follow him. Our call may not be as dramatic as theirs but the call is the same. Baptism in Jesus Christ means both death and life. Forgiveness is the Christlike suffering which is the Christian's duty to bear. We suffer together and we suffer for those whom we wish to follow Christ.

Chapter 41

THE HOLY SPIRIT IN THE LIVES OF GOD'S PEOPLE

The Holy Spirit is a person not an 'it.' He is the third person of the Trinity. Dr. John F. Walvoord of Dallas Seminary states: "The use of personal pronouns affirms personality of the Holy Spirit. Such as I, thou, he are used of persons. In the New Testament Greek the word pneuma is neuter and would normally take a neuter pronoun, but in fact the masculine pronouns are used." (John 15:26; 16:13-14) The pronouns refer to a person. We must understand him as a real personality, he is a divine person, One with the Father and the Son, worthy to receive our adoration, worship, praise and entitled to receive our entire surrender to him. We have to make this clear in our minds and hearts that he deserves our faith, our trust and our total surrender. Jesus Christ sent the Comforter to be with us to be at our side and to finish God's work here on earth. The Holy Spirit is the personal object of our faith.

Dr. John F. Walvoord, one of the most prominent evangelical scholars of his generation, (died 2010), wrote this about the Holy Spirit: "The personality of the Holy Spirit has been subjected to denial and neglect through the centuries of the Christian church and is seldom understood by twentieth century Christians." The Holy Spirit is more than some mysterious wonder and power that we, in our weakness and doubt only think of as a possible being out there in the ethers. The question we need to ask ourselves is how can I get to know the Holy Spirit and let his power influence me?

The heretic Arius believed the Holy Spirit was only the "exerted energy of God." This was repudiated at the Nicene Council in 325 A.D. Socinius and his followers in the sixteenth century held that the Holy Spirit was merely the eternally proceeding energy of God. This belief laid the foundation for modern Unitarianism. Unitarians deny the Trinitarian doctrine. Universalism believes all souls will be saved. Jehovah Witnesses believe Jesus Christ is not part of God and they have their own translation of the Bible. This belief system ties in with the belief of Arian Supremacy in Germany under Hitler's reign of terror. He tried to come up with the perfect race; the Arian race. The Mormons have their own bible, a product of founder, Joseph Smith. It is said that Thomas Jefferson made his own bible to fit his own beliefs. These different doctrines seem close to coming under the heading of cults.

To know and understand the ministry of the Holy Spirit from the biblical point of view is to believe in his divine nature and allow his Spirit to take over our life. There are those who brag about having received the Holy Spirit in their lives and are puffed up. They think they are something special. They are merely full of spiritual pride and arrogance. Anyone who has been touched by the Holy Spirit is filed with humility and love. Being boastful and proud is not what it means to be filled with the Holy Spirit. The opposite takes place. One is humbled, broken and blessed that God should allow his Spirit to engulf one's life to the fullest, to take possession of ones life and turn them into a useful vessel for Jesus Christ. Over the centuries thousands of God's children have experienced the Holy Spirit in their life.

It is my practice now that I am retired to go to the gym every day. I walk two to three miles every time and I have a routine doing seven different lifting exercises every other day to keep my muscle tone. How did all this come about? I started this routine over sixty years ago. I would take time from my duties as a pastor to keep fit. I have never stopped. The same thing applies to our life in the Holy Spirit; the moment we become Christians (regardless of our age) we receive the Holy Spirit. We are babes in Christ Jesus. From that moment on we begin to grow through the reading of the Word. The Holy Spirit guides us into all truth. Just like staying fit year after year we continue to grow and grow and grow with the guidance of the Holy Spirit. We are led to serve Jesus Christ with our talents and gifts. Our old ways of life gradually drop off and we follow Christ. The church is full of all kinds of gifts and talents the Holy Spirit is ready to put to work. He is ready to show us what gifts we have. It is for us to allow them to translate into meaningful opportunities.

In politics the president has to abide by the constitution. When he speaks he is backed by the authority of his office. He cannot go off willy-dilly and make decisions that ignore Congress or the Constitution. He has to be in check. The same idea applies when we come to the Bible. The prophets speak their VOICE , the apostles speak their VOICE, the disciples speak their VOICE and when Christ speaks his VOICE his words go forth with the power and authority of God. Their voices speak forth God's Word and we listen and obey. The Holy Spirit is sent to convince and convict the world of sin and judgment.

On the day of Pentecost the Holy Spirit came to be by their side to guide and to empower them for service. Jesus has not left us orphans. The great commission is not just for pastors or missionaries or certain special people, it is for all who call upon the name of the Lord. (Mathew 28:19-20) The Holy Spirit is our advocate, our counselor and our personal guide to the truth.

We are reminded that the Holy Spirit understands us. Dr. Torrey points out four distinctive characteristics of personality that are ascribed to the Holy Spirit and these are the same attributes in Christ. These characteristics are marks of personality — knowledge, feeling, emotion and will. This does not translate as we may think to hands, feet, eyes, ears and mouth. These things are about corporeality. I Corinthians 2:10,11: "But God has revealed them to us by His Spirit: for the Spirit searches the deep things of God. For what man knows the things of man, save the spirit of man which is in him? Even so the things of God no man knows but the Spirit of God." To paraphrase, this passage means the Holy Spirit knows the truth, is the truth.

In I Corinthians 12:11 we read: "...But all these worketh the self same Spirit, dividing to every man severally as He wills." Here the Bible is ascribing knowledge and truth and will to the Holy Spirit. This is not a power we try to control in order to get what we want. It is the power of God working through the Holy Spirit. It is not my will, but thy will be done. It is the deep things of God we seek. This Holy Person, the Holy Spirit, seeks to take possession of our lives and make us fit for the Master's use. In Romans 8:27: "And He that searches the hearts knows the mind of the Spirit, because He makes intercession for the saints according to the will of God."

The Greek word 'mind' translates 'ideas of thought, feelings and purpose.' In Romans 8:7 we read: "The carnal mind is enmity against God: for it is not subject to the law of God, neither indeed can be." John MacArthur points out that this enmity is of unbelievers and goes deeper than acts of disobedience. No matter how pious a person may appear his basic orientation is toward self-gratification. In I Corinthians 2:14 we read: "The natural person does not accept the things of the Spirit of God, for they are folly to him, and he is not able to understand them because they are spiritually discerned." "And He that searches the hearts knows the mind of the Spirit, because He intercedes for the saints according to the will of God."—Romans 8:27

I am not trying to make it appear that one knows something special about how God works. I am merely stating what the scriptures say; when one accepts Christ he comes alive in the Spirit of God. God gives him a new nature. If you haven't accepted these truths you are missing out on God's greatest gift of love.

Love is ascribed to the Holy Spirit. 'For the love of the Spirit,' we are to work together. (Romans 15:30). The same Greek word for love used here is he same one used for love of the Father and the Son. Stop and think for a moment about the importance of God's love. It is uniquely different than the verb 'agapao' which is used to also mean love. Before Christ the word *love* was used in secular Greek, it was colorless and without any great depth of meaning. The biblical writers used this form to describe many forms of love. The word 'agape' signifies the true meaning of the love of God to his dear Son. (John 17:26; Galatians 6:10, Heb.12:6). It is this love of God that prompts our obedience to him. (Mounce) When we realize what this great love of God has accomplished for us we will fall on our knees and worship him in reverential fear. For we know without his love and mercy we all would be headed straight to hell.

Chapter 42

MIRACLE OF MIRACLES

C hrist Jesus gave his life as ransom —the penalty and price that God required to remove guilt and sin— for the many who would be saved. The word 'ransom' means a payment for the redemption or freedom of a person. Under the Old Testament law and Judaism one could *ransom* a condemned person from execution by offering something valuable for his life. In the New Testament we see that Jesus Christ did what no one else could do by offering his life for the sin of the world. (John 3:16) Therefore the price for our forgiveness is paid in full. It is difficult for us to understand what it means when the Bible says Jesus Christ died for us and as Jesus said on the cross: "it is finished." He meant the full price, the ransom, was paid for our sins...finished! When you own a house you usually have a large mort- gage on it that has to be paid in increments each month. After years you sell the house, pay off any balance due and close the sale. You take a deep sigh of relief...it is finished. I owe nothing. Jesus Christ paid in full the price to redeem us—"it is finished." Believe it.

Listen how John's gospel describes the Father and the Son: "and the Word was made flesh, and dwelt among us, and we beheld his glory, the glory of the ONLY BEGOTTEN of the Father. Full of grace and truth." The words 'begotten' or 'beget' are hard to understand their full meaning today, but the best translation is in the idea of "THE ONLY BELOVED ONE." It carries singular uniqueness, one of a kind, beloved like no one else. It signals the character of the relationship between the Father and the Son in the Godhead." (John MacArthur commentary: John 3:16; 18; I John 4:9) God the Father and God the Son sent the Holy Spirit.

At Jesus' baptism the Holy Spirit descended upon him. John the Baptist was baptizing all the people in the river. Jesus came to him and requested to be baptized. At first John hesitated but Jesus reminded him it was necessary "for us to fulfill all righteousness." And immediately the heavens opened and "he saw the Spirit of God descending as a dove and coming upon Him and behold, a voice from the heavens saying, "This is my beloved Son, in whom I Am well pleased."—Matthew 3:16,17 This is repeated in Luke 3: 21, 22. Following his baptism Jesus began his public ministry. Here the Holy Spirit is separate and distinct from God the Father and Jesus Christ. The Holy Spirit indwelt Christ throughout his entire public ministry. When Jesus Christ went to John the Baptist to be baptized he came up out of the water with the Holy Spirit that was sent by the Father. I do not have any specific scripture to support my belief that we can conclude the Holy Spirit became "humanized" in Jesus Christ. By that I mean just as Jesus went to the cross and suffered and died for the remission of our sins so were the Holy Spirit and the Father there beside him.

In a sense God the Father looked away at the cross, could not look on sin and thus Jesus' words: "My God, My God, why have you forsaken Me?" The Scriptures show the Holy Spirit's work as Christ leaves the disciples to to be with the Father. He declares: "Father if it be thy will let this cup (the cup of death) pass from Me; never the less, not my will, but thine be done." –Luke 22:42 The entire time of Jesus' public ministry he lived and worked in the power of the Holy Spirit. Jesus was tempted in all areas of his life. Therefore, he learned even as our great High Priest, to sympathize with all our weaknesses.

There is a clear distinction between the Father, the Son and the Holy Spirit. The great commission in Matthew 28:19: "Go therefore and teach all nations, baptizing them in the name of the Father, and of the Son, and of the Holy Ghost." In John 14:6 Jesus says: "I will pray the Father, and He shall give you another Comforter, that He may abide with you forever." In John 16:7 we hear Jesus: "Nevertheless I tell you the truth; it is expedient for you that I go away: for if I go not away, the Comforter will not come unto you; but if I depart, I will send Him unto you."

There is the subordination of the Holy Spirit to the Father and the Son. Remember how often Jesus made the statement during his public ministry that he only does what his Father instructs. "I can of my own self do nothing but what my Father does."—John 5:30 Here Jesus is subordinate to the Father: "For I did not speak on my own initiative, but the Father Himself who sent

Me has given Me commandment, what to say, and what to speak. And I know that His commandment is eternal life: therefore the things I speak, I speak just as the Father has told me." — John 12:49-50.

Before we can acknowledge the Holy Spirit we need to make sure we understand who he is as a person in relation to the Father and the Son. Is he a Divine Person and if so does he deserve our utmost attention and worship? Should our lives be surrendered to him as the Father and Son commands us to receive him? He belongs to the Godhead, the third person of the Trinity. Is he worthy to receive our adoration, our faith, our love and our entire surrender to him? Do I believe the Holy Spirit is possessed with all the divine attributes of deity; omnipotence (all powerful), omniscience (all knowing), omnipresence (all presence)?

As Dr. Torrey says, the question is not '*how can I get more of the Holy Spirit?* but rather in the Biblical way as Divine Person, '*how can the Holy Spirit have more of me?*' The Holy Spirit intercedes on behalf of God's children. Romans 8:27 says: "And He that searches the heavens knows what is the mind of the Spirit, because He makes intercession for the saints according to the will of God." Here the Father and the Spirit and the Son are in agreement with what the Spirit thinks. Romans Vs. 28 makes this clear: "God causes all things to work together for good..." This is the providence of God at work. This is the foreknowledge of God. He is absolutely sovereign in all his actions and will. Look at Psalm 139:7-20 to see that omnipresence is ascribed to the Holy Spirit. In the Old Testament the Holy Spirit is sent to speak to different individuals to command specific tasks to be performed.

Dr. Torrey points out that at least twenty-five different names are used in the Old and New Testament when referring to the Holy Spirit. The simplest name-is the Spirit. The Hebrew and Greek words for the Holy Spirit translated include: "Breath" or "Wind" (Gen. 2:7; John 20:22). "He breathed on them…"Thou dost send forth Thy Spirit, and they are created."—Job 33:4 "The Spirit of God hath made me, and the breath of the Almighty hath given me life."—Job 33:4 These passages show the outpouring of the breath of God. The Holy Spirit quickens the life of the believer and dwells in a personal way in all his glory and divinity. You have God at your side as it were. This is the whole ministry of the Comforter. The Greek word is 'paraclete' or Comforter, one who is in you and guides your life. He brings peace to the soul. Do you fully comprehend this truth?

The Holy Spirit of God gives wisdom and endows people with abilities for leadership, abilities they never thought they had before. In the building of the Tabernacle the Holy Spirit told Moses how it was to be built by naming all the different materials and identifying the seamstress and die makers to complete the work. (Exodus 31:2, 35:35:31; Nehemiah 9:20). God's Spirit enabled ordinary people to win battles against formidable foes. (Judges 6:6:34. 13:25, 14:6, 19,15:14). The Holy Spirit gave divine revelation to prophets. (Ezekiel 13:3)(Mounce)

Nicodemus came to Jesus by night to question his power and authority. Nicodemus admitted Jesus must be from God because no man could do the things he did unless he was from God. Jesus immediately directed Nicodemus' attention to the truth. Here we have the importance of the Holy Spirit: "That which is born of the flesh, is flesh; that which is born of the Spirit is Spirit. Marvel not that I said unto thee, you must be born again. The wind blows where it chooses, and you hear the sound thereof, but canst not tell where it came from, and where it goes next, so is every one that is born of the Spirit."—John 3:6-8. The word 'wind' could be used in both places. Wind is used to describe the Holy Spirit. He is sovereign we cannot dictate to him. (I Corinthians 12:11) but we are called upon to submit ourselves and our wills absolutely to his sovereign will.

The sovereign Spirit of God will work through us and accomplish his own work by using us to carry out God's will. The Spirit of God is invisible and we may feel he is not there for us but he is. The world will know we are walking by the Spirit as we walk by faith and not by sight. We will feel the breath of the wind upon our cheeks, we will feel his breath upon our souls, and we will witness the mighty things he does. (R. A. Torrey)

Many times we felt the wind blowing off the Pacific in San Francisco and in Carmel, California. When we drove home recently from a trip to California we had to drive through three states where the wind was blowing forty miles per hour. It shook our car from side to side. We had to hold tight on the steering wheel to keep it from pushing us off the roadway. The Spirit, like the wind is independent. It has been said that the five healthiest cites are located around lakes. It is because the wind blowing from the lakes brings life and health. When the Holy Spirit comes and blows into our hearts, he brings new life to the soul. We breathe the fresh air of spiritual freedom.

Chapter 43

THE HOLY SPIRIT AND THE LIFE OF THE CHURCH

The Holy Spirit brings new life to the Church and a community. In John 6:63 we read: "...it is the Spirit that gives life." In Ezekiel' story of the dry bones, there was no life until the wind blew and suddenly these bones came alive. There are numerous true stories where the Holy Spirit visited and great revivals broke out. Read the stories of Jonathan Edwards, and Dwight L. Moody, and of course Dr. Billy Graham.

The Holy Spirit is called the Spirit of Christ. In Romans 8:9 we read: "But you are not in the flesh, but in the Spirit, if so be that the Spirit of God dwell in you. Now, if any man has not the Spirit of Christ, he is none of His." He is called the Spirit of Christ because he is Christ's gift. John 14:15: "It was necessary for Christ to go to be with the Father so He could send the Spirit. To His disciples He said, and I will ask the Father and He will give you another Comforter, Advocate that He may remain with you forever."—John14:16. "The Spirit of

Truth, Whom the world cannot receive, because it does not see Him, nor know or recognize Him, for He lives with you and will be in you," (Vs.17); "I will not leave you orphans…" (Vs.18)

The Holy Spirit was imparted to the disciples following the resurrection appearances of Jesus Christ. Many writers say they did not receive the Holy Spirit until Pentecost but according to John 20:22f Jesus breathed on them and said to them "receive (admit) the Holy Spirit." And having received the Holy Spirit, and being led by Him, they went forth to witness and declare the forgiveness of sins to all who believed. Their fear, anxiety and apprehension were replaced with joy. They returned to Jerusalem with great joy in the Holy Spirit (Lk.24:52; Rom. 14:1). So, what is the event at Pentecost? Arthur Pink says that at Pentecost the power of baptism was received. This was needed for them to speak in tongues to the multitudes of Jews who came from every country under heaven. (Acts 2:1-5ff)

The Holy Spirit has been sent to reveal everything about Christ. "He shall bear witness of Me."—John 15:26. In Ephesians 3:16,17: "Paul's prayer that the Father would grant to believers according to the riches of His glory to be strengthened with might by His Spirit in the inner man, that Christ might dwell in their hearts by faith." This is the ministry of the Holy Spirit. In the process of my reading several books on this important subject, I gained good introspection. A. W. Tozer gave this important insight: "to a large degree familiarity has brought boredom to the evangelical church, especially in America. We have heard the same thing repeated over and over again until we are bored…we are dying by degrees because we are forgetting that there is a Spirit of the Word without which the truth of the Word means nothing to the human spirit." Tozer remarks: "God has put everlasting into our souls."

"The Holy Spirit searches all things, yea, and the deep things of God. For who among men knows the things of a men, save the spirit of man which is in him? Even so the things of God none knows, save the Spirit of God."—Corinthians 2:10-11

He is the Spirit of wisdom and understanding (Epesians 1:17)
He is the Spirit of counsel and might
He is the Spirit of knowledge of the fear of the Lord. (Isaiah 11:2)
His sensitivity is revealed in that the Spirit can be grieved by sin (Ephesians 4:30)
The Holy Spirit has a personality (Dr. Valvoord)

Dr. Torrey points out over twenty-five different ways the Holy Spirit is revealed. Time will only allow us to mention a few. I recommend you get a copy of his book for personal study. The Holy Spirit is the Spirit of life.

This passage is Messianic: "Then a shoot will spring from the stem of Jesse (Jesse was David's father), and a branch from the roots will bear fruit. And the Spirit of the Lord will rest upon Him, the spirit of wisdom and under- standing, the spirit of counsel and strength, the spirit of knowledge and the fear of the Lord."—Isaiah 11:1-2

"As the Spirit rested upon David as king, so it will rest upon Christ, ruler of the world."(MacArthur)

John 6:63: "It is the Spirit who gives life; the flesh profits nothing; the words that I have spoken to you are spirit and are life." John 14-17 is the most powerful message by Jesus Christ. These chapters in the Gospel of John should be read whenever we become lonely or fearful about our life or are faced with painful trials and tribulation. Comforting verse:

- The Holy Spirit (the pnuma) Greek is also our Comforter (parakaleo), our guide into all truth. This is a powerful statement direct from the mouth of our Lord Jesus Christ to his disciples. Jesus was about to leave them to go to the Father. They suddenly felt fearful and abandoned. This is a wonderful message to all of us who have ever faced fear of abandonment.

- When feeling loneliness or fear John, chapter 14 is one of the great chapters of comfort and love from the heart of Jesus Christ and the Holy Spirit. Read it over and over and over again. When my first wife Dorothy died of cancer these passages brought peace and comfort to my soul.

- What does it mean to BELIEVE? It means that not only our salvation and future home is in heaven, but also the peace we have here on earth and knowing Jesus Christ, our savior, is here for us."...let not your heart be troubled, believe in God, believe also in Me." What a caring statement he leaves his disciples.

- Vs. 15: "If you love Me, you will keep my commandments." Vs. 16: "And I will ask the Father, and He will give you another Helper, that He may be with you forever. That is the Spirit of truth" *How long? Forever.* Vs.18: "I WILL NOT LEAVE YOU ORPHANS, I will come to you." Then in Chapter 16:7 ff. we read: "I tell you the truth, it is to your advantage that I go away; for if I do not go away, the Helper shall not come to you. And when He comes, he will convict the world concerning sin and righteousness and judgment; sin they do not believe in Me..."

The Holy Spirit is the Spirit of truth. Jesus said when he comes he will guide us into all truth. The Holy Spirit will not speak of his own initiative, but whatever he hears (from the Father and the Son) he will speak; and he will disclose to us what is to come. The Holy Spirit shall glorify God.

John vs.14, 15: "Soak up these words. Jesus said, I AM the way the truth and the life, no man can come to the Father but by Me." The Holy Spirit was sent to verify this truth and bring the message to bear on every heart and mind. In John 14:16, Jesus reminds his disciples: "...he will ask the Father and he will give them the Advocate, One who will come and stand by your side. He will fill you with power." And the Holy Spirit remains with the disciples forever until Jesus returns.

The Holy Spirit takes part in removing (cleansing) sin in our lives. When you have the Holy Spirit you will give up sin, narcissistic or selfish desires, hatred, and anger. He will replace these with love, joy, peace, patience, kindness. This doesn't mean we will never sin again but it means we have an advocate who helps us overcome sin. The holy attributes of Christ will begin to fill our hearts and minds. The deeper you go into the study of

Christ's life the more you will want to become like him. In Romans 8:26-28: "The importance of earthly things will begin to become less and less important and the things of the Spirit of God will become all consuming in our hearts and minds."

Perhaps some of you are thinking this is easy for older people to accept because they have lived a large portion of their lives. As young people we have much to live for—our jobs, our marriage, our raising of children, enjoyment of just living life to the fullest. It is like saying I am not ready yet to give my full life's commitment and my will over to God. How old was John the Baptist? How old were the Apostles and all those who witnessed the Pentecost? They were of all ages.

This is just one of the reasons why the Spirit of God and the VOICE of God is dead in our churches. We love to play church on Sunday mornings and then go back into the world where everything but God is more important. Ask yourself these questions: Do you think God is not interested in living in your entire life, day-by-day? Can one get along without God's presence to guide and to direct your life? The world is completely oblivious to the power of the Holy Spirit in our world. They will find out too late if the Christians were suddenly taken out at the Rapture.

When I pastored a church in California I had a number of opportunities to counsel and work with people who had difficulty giving up their various habits holding them back from going all out for Jesus Christ. They understood what their problem was but found it almost impossible to surrender to the good in themselves. This prevented them from following Christ. The promise God's Word comes through in Mathew 6:33: "He will not tempt you above what you are able, but with the temptation provide a way through it." The victory is yours. Through the testing and trials of life we become stronger.

The Lord called me early—I was 26 yrs. old—to begin a ministry in San Francisco. Before founding my church I held several positions of leadership at our church in Oakland, California. The Lord can call us at any age. It is important to heed his call. The Holy Spirit will lead us. Of course I was very immature but I walked by faith trusting in God. Romans 8:27: "…and He who searches the hearts knows what the mind of the Spirit is, because He intercedes for the saints according to the will of God." The Holy Spirit equipped Dorothy and me for service in San Francisco eighty years ago.

The Holy Spirit is sent by Jesus Christ to continue his work of bringing men and women to salvation and discipleship. His work is that of convicting and convincing the world of sin because they do not believe in Jesus Christ. That is the major sin. In John 16:8-11 Jesus reminds his disciples the importance of his going to be with the Father. "If he does not go the Helper (Holy Spirit) will not come. But if I go I will send Him to you." "…And He, when He comes will convict the world of sin, and righteousness and of judgment."

He will convict the world universal, all encompassing: Of sin because He has come and the world has rejected their only hope, Jesus Christ. Many religions have their gods who they worship, but there is only One true God, Jesus Christ our Lord.

*Of righteousness, Jesus is the only righteous-
ness One,
Of Judgment, because the devil has been judged.
All Judgment has been put in Christ's hands. .*

The Holy Spirit is sent to bear witness of Jesus Christ.
John 15:26: "When the Helper comes whom I will send
to you from the Father, that is the Spirit of truth, who proceeds from the Father, He will bear witness of Me." Here
we see the Father, the Son and the Holy Spirit working
together. Because the disciples have born witness of
Jesus Christ, they will soon be empowered with the Holy
Spirit to bear witness beside them. In Acts 5:32, Peter
speaks before the Council: "… and we are witnesses of
these things; and so is the Holy Spirit, whom God has
given to those who obey Him." The Holy Spirit's work
is not complete unless those who are saved become true
and living disciples of Jesus Christ.

Making sure we pray according to His will. When
we pray in the name of the Lord Jesus Christ to bring
conviction on those with whom we are involved in their
salvation, do we ask that the Holy Spirit do His work as
Jesus said, to convict and convince of sin? We end our
prayers almost always by saying, *'in Jesus' name, amen.'*
Shouldn't we say *'in Jesus' name by His Holy Spirit?'*
On the day of Pentecost over 3,000 people were saved.
This was the work of the Holy Spirit convicting men and
women of their sin of rejecting Jesus Christ. Can this
moving of the "Wind" happen today? How? It happens
when God's people take God seriously and pray earnestly
for the outpouring of the Holy Spirit in their midst.

There is regenerating work of the Holy Spirit. Paul in Titus 3:5 states: "It is not by works of righteousness, which we did ourselves, but according to His mercy He saved us, through the washing of regeneration and renewing of the Holy Spirit." Here we see it is the Holy Spirit that renews us daily.

Regeneration is the imputation of new life. Every day we should begin by asking the Holy Spirit to fill us anew with his power, his wisdom and his righteousness in Jesus name. Amen. Before we became a Christian we were dead in trespasses and sins. It is by God's grace alone that we are saved. "For by grace are you saved and that not of yourselves, it is a (free) gift of God."— Ephesians 2:8. Man can't do anything to earn it or to save himself; it is all by God's mercy.

The Holy Spirit comes and imparts new life into the heart and soul. This takes us back to what I said about the importance of knowing the written Word of God. The Holy Spirit teaches and imparts God's truths to our minds. The more we know God's Word the more the Holy Spirit has to work with. Spiritual things are spiritually discerned and without the Spirit of God, you cannot understand the things of God. It's that simple and yet so profound. In II Corinthians 3:6, we read: "...the letter (of the law or of stone) kills but the Spirit gives life." The Holy Spirit has a personality just like God. That is why he communicates to us like God communicates with us.

Why was the law so important in the Bible?

Except for the law I would not have known I was a sinner. The law served its purpose. The law kills and brings death, but the Spirit brings new life.

Regeneration is the implantation of a new nature imputation in us. The old life is gone and the new life begins. We are a new creation in Christ Jesus. When we are saved we become alive in Christ Jesus, a new creation. We feel the fire and witness of the Holy Spirit within. We want to tell everyone what has happened to us. We want to devour the word of God, as the Scriptures say we hunger for spiritual food. Why does the fire seem to die out after while? We return to our old way of life with all its temptations and demands.

Has the Holy Sprit left us? Is the Holy Spirit asleep? Is there such a thing as a second work of grace waiting to zap us? What does the Scripture say? The old sinning nature is still around to dog our tracks. It razes its ugly head when we least expect it to happen. How do we handle these situations? We have a strong advocate in the Holy Spirit. Claim his promise to deliver you. Resist the devil and he will flee from you. The devil especially hates hymns about Jesus. With the will perverted we think only of those things that bring us worldly plea- sure. We are out of harmony with God. The new man in harmony with God seeks the fruits of the Spirit; love, joy, peace. "Long suffering, gentleness, meekness, good- ness and temperance; against such there is no law." — Galatians 5:22,23; I Corinthians 13

This brings us to the Spiritual gifts of the Holy Spirit. If you talk to Christians about where they are in their spiritual journey and ask what their gifts or gift is–their answer will surprise you. '*What gifts? I don't have time for gifts, I am very busy. My life is taken up with work, family, friends, children, golf, fishing and boating.*' What do you think about these answers now that you have come this far in the study of the Holt Spirit? God does not deny these things but they must not control one's life.

GOD MUST BE IN FIRST PLACE.

We begin with GOD'S VOICE in the morning and we conclude our day in prayer with him as we lay our head down on the pillow. "Seek first the kingdom of God. Worship God with all your heart, with your entire mind and with your soul." Jesus told Satan, "You shall worship the Lord your God, and serve Him only."—Mathew 4:10. "Where your treasure is there you will find your heart fastened on."—Mathew 6:21 You cannot be double minded, James tells followers of Jesus Christ. The gift God gives us is his seal upon us. It is to be used for his glory and honor. Read good books that will help you in your walk with the Lord. I recommend A.W. Tozer and *Forgotten God: Reversing Our Tragic Neglect of the Holy Spirit* by Francis Chan and Danae Yankoski. These books will guide and encourage your faith.

What are the Gifts For? Now, let's examine at the different gifts of the Holy Spirit. In I Corinthians 14:1,4;12 Paul cautions us: "Prophecy is the supreme gift, tongues is not. The greatest gift of all is LOVE." Speaking in tongues is useless unless it is done to edify the body of Christ. Otherwise one should keep silent. Prophecy edifies the church. With tongues the person gets the center of attention, is puffed up and only edifies himself not the church. We see how the influence and power of the Holy Spirit works in the life of the Christian in I Corinthians 12th chapter: "Now there are varieties of gifts, but the same God who works all things in all persons. But each one is given the manifestation of the

Spirit for the common good. "There are verities of gifts and the same Spirit, and there are various ministries and the same Lord, and there are verities of effects, but it is the same God who works all things in all persons, but each one is given the manifestation of the Spirit for the common good..."

Chapter 44

WHY DO WE NEED
THE CHURCH?

W hy do we need the church? I can go out into
nature and worship God. I do not need the church
and their constant pressure of passing the offering plate.
I don't need the fellowship of other people to keep
me propped up. I can seek God on my own terms that
way I am not accountable to anyone but myself. These
are some excuses people use for not obeying the Lord.
Don't get me wrong, I agree that many churches are busy
entertainers. They do whatever is necessary to bring in
the crowds and produce mega churches. I would like the
opportunity to preach a few weeks from their pulpits and
go through the book of Romans with them. Paul deals
with true discipleship and obedience to the will of God.
It would be interesting to get their response.

The Holy Spirit calls for repentance for sin to be
removed from the life all that are ungodly. Preaching
the true gospel is costly to everyone who believes.
If you don't think so study carefully the life of Paul,

read his Epistles. You will find that God's grace comes with a price. Study Romans. Also read good books like Bonhoeffer's *Cost of Discipleship* and C. S. Lewis' books. Study deeply the Bible and listen for God's voice to speak to you personally. "Ask and you will receive, seek and you will find, knock and the door will be opened to you."—Matthew 21:22 ASK.

We are entering into a period of history and life that indicates the world powers are coming to a head. There is more uncertainty and chaos in our world than in the last fifty years. This could be the sign of God bringing man to the end his days. Keep an eye on the events taking place in Israel and the Middle East where there is constant unrest and violence. Why is this whole area so set on the inhabitation of Israel? Today we have 'the little satin' and the 'big satin.' Morality and civility are at an all time low in America.

What are the signs of Christ's return? In the last days there will be deceivers and false Christs. Jesus already warned us about this. He also said in the last days there will be famine, pestilences, earthquakes in different places, nation shall fight against each other, the sun and the moon will turn into blood, and men will be lovers of pleasure rather than lovers of God. These are the beginning death throes. Christians will be persecuted because of their faith in Jesus Christ. And false prophets shall rise up and deceive many.

Listen to what Matthew says about the last days. Matthew 24:4ff: "And Jesus answered and said...you will be hearing of wars and rumors of war, see that you are not frightened, for these things must take place, but that is not the end. For nation will rise against nation...

there will be famines and earthquakes, but all these things are merely the beginning of birth pangs." He continues in verse 4: "See to it that no one misleads you, for many will come using my name declaring they are the Christ....try the spirits whether they are true or false." In order for us to be ready we need to know God's Word. Don't take anything for granted. It is time to be prepared.

There will be those who give up their faith and will be deceived. BUT those who remain steadfast, unmovable and endure to the end shall be saved. Matthew 24:7ff: "The Christian shall receive the crown of life and a new name will be given to them. Amen, praise the Lord." Until Christ returns for us we must give ourselves very diligently to the reading and mastering the WORD, which is God's revelation. Colossians 3:16: Let the WORD of Christ dwell in you richly in all wisdom; teaching and admonishing one another in psalms and hymns and spiritual song, singing with grace in your hearts to the Lord."

When the early church was formed it was a house church where believers who had recently accepted Christ after hearing the Apostles. They gathered together and sang hymns, prayed together, listened to the word and had fellowship. They willingly gave out of the abundance of their hearts what was needed to take care of widows and orphans and the sick. They supported each other in following Christ. This is why the church is important. Have you gone to church lately? This might be the right time for you to let Jesus Christ speak to your heart.

In Dr. David Levy's book *Gray Matter*, he talks about the first time he decided he had to go to church: "I was going through a personal transformation, I still believed, stubbornly and arrogantly, that I didn't need a church. I liked my individual approach. I didn't see why church was necessary, at least for me. Playing volleyball or surfing was my "church." There was another reason I avoided it—Fear. I was still living in my identity as a Jewish doctor. I still attended synagogue. I wanted to have a private relationship without threatening my professional reputation or my social relationships. Finally I summoned my nerve one Sunday morning and drove to a nearby church. I sat in the parking lot, consumed with fear." For a few moments he thought over all the reasons he should not go in and then, pushing his fears aside he walked in and participated in his first Christian church service in twenty years. Later he said, "...the fellowship with others who followed Jesus became an important part of my life." Get this book and read it. You will laugh, you will cry, you will read it several times. My wife Sharon and I have read it through three times so far.

The question we need to be asking ourselves today-*where are the gifts*? The church is where the gifts are to be used to edify the body of Christ yet we see very little of the gifts being manifested in the church. Why is this? Every born again Christian has his own gift given to him/her by the Holy Spirit. It is to be used for the edification of the body of Christ. No one holds a special place of privilege over another person.

It is our responsibility to know what our gift is and invest it in the work of ministry in the church saving souls. Just think for a moment what would happen in the church and the world if every person would allow their gift to flourish for the glory of God? "You shall find Me when you search for Me with all your heart." Jeremiah 29:13 In the church the witness of the Holy Spirit is a diminishing effect. But this could change if people began allowing the Holy Spirit his freedom to work the opposite effect. The result? The body of Christ would flourish.

The Scriptures make it clear the importance of every believer setting aside his/her own desires and dreams of power to work for the Holy Spirit. The church will prosper when we begin asking God to forgive us of our preconceived ideas and desires and begin praying for each other. Our gifts do not get lost in a vacuum. If one member suffers we all suffer. We are to bear one another's burden. I Corinthians 12,13: "All the abilities are inspired and brought together by the Holy Spirit, who gives to each individual as HE chooses."

At age 21, Dietrich Bonhoeffer wrote his doctoral thesis on *The Communion of Saints*. I would like to share some of his thoughts that are as important today as when he first penned them in 1927. "The Church owes its existence to Jesus Christ. Without His presence in the actualization in the Church, it cannot exist. This place is given to him through the word, impelled by the Spirit of the crucified and risen Lord of the Church. The Spirit is capable of operating through the word: Christ is the Word. The word is his VOICE. The Holy Spirit operates solely in the church as the communion of the saints...It is by the grace of God that a congregation is permitted to gather visibly in this world to share God's Word and sacrament."

There are different opinions in theology and speculation as to what the Bible says concerning healing or tongues. Are they still in use and available today? Some reliable scholars believe these gifts ceased following the end of the apostolic ministry. They believe that they were necessary in ancient times to demonstrate the power and witness of Jesus Christ who was no longer present. The Holy Spirit is sent to fulfill Christ's work. But there are equally reliable scholars who believe these gifts are still alive and available today. The Pentecostal movement holds this view, but they are not alone. I recommend Francis Chan's book *The Forgotten God* to anyone who wants to understand how the Holy Spirit should work in a person's life. The nominal Christian has no idea what they are missing. Why is the Holy Spirit still the FORGOTTEN GOD? People are afraid to trust the Lord all the way for fear of what it may cost them; what they may have to give up.

Others haven't asked God to become Lord of their life. Then there are those who have not taken the time and prayer to study the Bible.

Here is Paul's list of the gifts:
- The word of wisdom
- The word of knowledge
- Faith by the same Spirit
- Gifts of healing by the same Spirit
- To another the effecting of miracles
- To another prophecy
- To another distinguishing of spirits
- To another various kinds of tongues

One and the same Spirit delivers all these gifts, distributing to each person individually just as HE WILLS. "The body is one and yet has many members of the body. Though they are many, yet they are one body in Christ."— 1 Corinthians 12:12 J.B. Phillips commentary reminds the believer to beware there are those in the church who are sickly and feeble, who are found spiritually asleep" (I Corinthians 11:30) The church is the ecclesia (body) of Christian fellowship. Having said all this the greatest gift is LOVE. Make it your ambition to acquire it.

From the late Dr. A. W. Tozer, editor of the *Alliance Witness* for many years:

"We may as well face it: the whole level of spirituality among us is low. We have measured ourselves by ourselves until the incentive to seek higher pleasures in the things of the Spirit is all but gone. We have imitated the world, sought popular favor, manufactured delights to substitute for the joy the Lord and produced a cheap and synthetic power to substitute for the power of the Holy Spirit."

Who is in control of these gifts? WHO? WHO? WHO? The Holy Spirit. He alone decides what our gift shall be. A word of wisdom: "If a man lacks wisdom, let him ask of God, who gives to all men generously, and without reproach, and it will be given him. BUT let him ask in faith, without doubting…"—James 1:5,6; I Corinthians 12:11. READ James 1:5-6 for God's revelation makes known his truth: "You shall know the truth and the truth will set you free." Faith by the same Spirit: faith comes by hearing the truth, studying faithfully God's Word and eating it as a daily diet. A confident trust in God develops in the heart, mind and soul as one commits to the Lord in obedient persistency." Hebrews 11:1: "Faith is the substance of things hoped for, the evidence of things not seen." ASV says: "…the assurance of things hoped for, the conviction of things not seen."

The Holy Spirit heals. In James 5:13-16: "...any sick among you let him call for the elders of the church, and let them pray over them, anointing them with oil (symbol of the Holy Spirit) in the name of the Lord. And the prayer of faith will save him and the Lord will restore him; and if he has committed sins, he will be forgiven." This is part of the church's ministry today. The effective prayer of a 'righteous man' can accomplish much. Who is righteous? The person who lives his life in conformity to God's will. How do we look at this ministry of healing today? Each person has to decide what God's Word says about it. There are many instances of divine healing. I personally believe in divine healing.

My own life experience while in the hospital in California in 1996 is a testament to divine healing. I was suffering with bleeding ulcers. The doctors wanted to take out forty percent of my stomach. I asked my doctor who declared I needed this surgery to save my life to give me time for God to heal me. I prayed and prayed for God's healing hand to stop the bleeding. Miraculously, before they could operate, God healed me completely. Was this a miracle? My doctor certainly had never seen such a spontaneous healing. In our culture today, people have a hard time believing in God let alone believing in divine healing. Miracles...what is a miracle? Jesus changed the water into wine. He walked on the water, he spoke to the waves and they obeyed his command. He healed the lame, the sick, the blind man and the leper. Look these instances up on your own and ask yourself the question: are these authentic? Can the Holy Spirit perform miracles today?

A miracle is when something happens to defy the natural laws of nature. The laws of nature are suspended in time. The key here is to never underestimate the power of God, the power of Jesus Christ and the power of the Holy Spirit. Be open to everything God has in mind to give you. *My faith looks up to thee, dear Lamb of Calvary, savior divine.*

Prophecy: in the Old Testament the word "naba" can mean to announce, or a spokesperson, or to bubble up, words of passion or under divine revelation. Others refer to it as being called, like the prophets of old. Jeremiah was called to be the prophet of Israel, he became known as the weeping prophet because he mourned for the sins of his people. In the New Testament the Greek word is "phophateuw" to predict the future, referring to the living presence of the Holy Spirit. It can be a gift of the Holy Spirit to someone for the purpose of building up the body of Christ; his church. Distinguishing of Spirits: the Bible says to try the spirits whether they be of God. This is discernment of spirits. It means being able to compare Scripture with Scripture and to discern false teaching. It keeps one from being misled. Study, study, study to show yourself approved of God. (Mathew 24:24)

Various kinds of tongues: Acts 2:4-12: "… given to the disciples to reach out to people of every tongue present with the good news of God's word." Can people speak in tongues today? Only where God allows it for the edification of the body of Christ, it is not for self-gratification. I Corinthians: "We are sealed by the Holy Spirit." (Ephesians 1:13-14 I Corinthians 6:19, 20): "Release the Holy Spirit in your life and let God reign and rule." Paul wrote to the Philippians church with these words: "…

have this attitude in yourselves which was also in Christ Jesus, who although He existed in the form of God, did not regard equality with God a thing to be grasped, but emptied Himself, taking on the form of a bond servant, and being made in the likeness of man, and being in the appearance of man, He humbled himself by becoming obedient to the point of death, even the death of the cross."

"Therefore, God highly exalted Him, and bestowed on Him, the name which is above every name, that the name of Jesus every knee should bow, of those who are in heaven and on earth, and under the earth, and every tongue should confess that Jesus Christ is Lord, to the glory of the Father... work out your own salvation with fear and trembling, for it is God who is at work in you, both to will to work for His good pleasure."—Philippians 2:5-13.

"SPIRIT OF THE LIVING GOD FALL AFRESH ON ME."

Dear God, I pray that whoever reads this material concerning the work and ministry of the Holy Spirit will understand the importance of the third Person of the Trinity, be set on fire, filled with the Holy Spirit and sanctified to go forth and proclaim your word, your voice to the world, in Jesus' name. Amen.

Part III

THE HOLY SPIRIT IS THE COMFORTER

Chapter 45

COMFORT IN THE MIDST
OF SUFFERING

P aul, the disciple of Jesus, reminds us there is always
comfort in the midst of suffering. All who believe in
Jesus Christ will suffer persecution in the last days. Jesus
warned his disciples: "If they persecuted me, they will
also persecute you.—John 15:20b. "Be of good cheer,
for I have overcome the world." John 16:33 Part three of
More Than Just Words studies the importance of allowing
the Holy Spirit to do his work of comforting those who
find themselves being persecuted and suffering for the
cause of Christ. The Christian is to comfort those who
may be suffering in ways and under circumstances they
had nothing to do to cause it happening to them.

In America today there is very little physical suffering
for faith in Jesus Christ. We have hardened ourselves to
deny or ignore the subject of suffering and religion. Two
things we shy away from are religion and politics. We
avoid them like the plague. Today we are politically correct in what we say to each other. If we stray from the

politically correct point of view we are labeled either bigots or just ill-informed. We often keep silent even within our own family groups because we don't want to hurt anyone's feelings. I will not stop praying for my entire family members to be saved.

In our society we avoid honest debates and discussions about things that may irritate or disagree with our personal perspective; worldview. *I guess it's better to let a person go to hell than to try and save them from it?* The only problem with this way of thinking is it's in direct violation with God's warnings in his Word. In John's Gospel we read why the Gospel was written in the first place; "These things are written that you may believe that Jesus is the Christ, the Son of God, and that believing you may have life in His name,"—John 20: 30-31.

Following his resurrection Jesus addresses his disciples with these words: "All authority has been given to Me in heaven and on earth. Go therefore and make disciples of all nations, baptizing them in the name of the Father and the Son and the Holy Spirit, teaching them to observe all that I commanded you." His promise, "I AM with you always, even to the end of the age."—Matthew 28:18-20.

I must remind my family, my friends and associates that based on what Jesus Christ has said is what I believe to be true, that I cannot do otherwise but be his witness. I have heard his voice speaking to me with his Word. I know his truth in my heart. My conscience will not allow me to do otherwise. If I am to suffer loss for my stand, so be it. I count all things but loss that I may know Christ and the fellowship of his suffering. (Philippians 3, the entire chapter).

Chapter 46

THE CHRISTIAN, THE CHURCH AND SUFFERING

In the book of Second Corinthians Paul admonishes Christians at Corinth to stand fast in their faith even in the midst of suffering. Suffering for Christ can take on many forms; they hated Jesus without cause as he was impeccable, without sin. They hated his words because his words were true. They would rather live a lie. They despised Jesus because he revealed the deepest secrets of their hearts. John the Baptist was beheaded, Peter was hung upside down on a cross and Stephen was stoned to death. In II Corinthians Paul tells of all his instances of persecution and suffering. II Corinthians 4:16-18: "We can say therefore, we do not lose heart, but though our outer man is decaying, yet our inner man is being renewed day by day."

In the very first chapter of II Corinthians Paul talks about how God sustains his children by faith. The word COMFORT is mentioned ten times in the first seven verses: "Blessed be the God and Father of our Lord Jesus

Christ, the Father of mercies and God of all comfort. Who comforts us in our entire affliction so that we may be able to comfort those who are in any affliction with the comfort with which we ourselves are comforted by God, for just as the sufferings are ours in abundance, so also our comfort is abundant through Christ. But if we are afflicted, it is for your comfort and salvation; or if we are comforted, it is for your comfort, which is effective in the patient enduring of the same sufferings which we also suffer. And our hope for you is firmly grounded, knowing that as you are sharers of our sufferings, so also you are sharers of our comfort."—II Corinthians 1:1-7. In this passage of Scripture Paul uses the word 'comfort' which is the same root Greek word 'paraklatos' meaning the Comforter, the Holy Spirit, one who comes to be at our side. Amen.

As you probably know by now Dietrich Bonhoeffer is my favorite theologian. He lived during the late thirties and early forties; during the Nazi Holocaust. He never relented in his Christian faith and because of his stand against Hitler and the German atrocities to the Jews he ultimately paid with his life by hanging for his part in the resistance movement and assassination attempt on Hitler's life. The National German Reich Church had absorbed the churches that succumbed to their ideology and were forced to display the Nazi Swastika over the cross in the sanctuary. He established the Finkenwald anti-Nazi Confessing Church. He brought a group of seminarians together for the purpose of preparing them for future ministry.

His works are unique because of his understanding of the interaction of religion, politics, and culture among the few Christians who opposed National Socialism. His writings have received international attention for over fifty years. The book *Life Together* was developed as a result of working with his seminary students who were preparing to go into the ministry during and following WWII. His *Cost of Discipleship* is a classic. *Life Together* has since gone through twenty-three printings. Thousands of people have purchased this little book since its first English printing in 1954. This powerful text is only 122 pages long but the serious Christian student, pastor or church leader who is interested in the ongoing quest for spiritual formation of the body of Christ finds inspiration and true discipline and discipleship in its pages. Bonhoeffer began with a few serious seminarians and he set out to guide and teach them what it meant to follow Jesus Christ. He gave his own life as a witness to what it meant to follow Christ. His *Cost of Discipleship* and *The Communion of Saints* are still being purchased today.

Bonhoeffer's title *Life Together* says exactly what it means; to develop his students into a family, a community of believers who are dedicated to following Christ as outlined in the Sermon on the Hill. These same commitments are a watchword; it is more than 'light for today.' It is God's revealed Word for all men, for all times. Being a member of the family involved following required commitments of each seminary student minister in training. They were to listen to God's VOICE by:

Reading of the word, listen for His VOICE speaking to you
Meditation, ask for wisdom and guidance to His truth

Prayer for His will to be done in your life
Communion—He is filling your heart with your
and peace, and joy
Service—Lord, lead me to obey your will

Bonhoeffer saw these same elements necessary for the growth and development of the true Christocentric church. I repeat his words, "It is by the grace of God that a congregation is permitted to gather visibly in this world to share God's Word and sacrament." Again," the sin of respectable people reveals itself in flight from responsibility"…"We belong to one another only through and in Jesus Christ. A Christian needs others because of Jesus Christ, and he comes to others through Jesus Christ and in Jesus Christ we have been chosen from eternity, accepted in time, and united for eternity."

Here is the most important reason why we should gather together in God's house; it is for our own benefit that we fellowship with others of like mind, who will follow the message of Jesus Christ. In these very trying and desperate days facing us, we need the assurance of hope and faith and trust in only one person who can save us: Jesus Christ. Scripture states: "…not forsaking the assembly of yourselves together, so much more as you see the day approaching."—Hebrews 10:19-25

From *Life Together, The Classic Exploration of Faith in Community* by Dietrich Bonhoeffer:

Since therefore, brethren, we have confidence to enter the
Holy place by the blood of Jesus, by a new and living way

*Which He inaugurated for us through the veil,
that is His flesh, and since we have a great priest
over the house of God, let us draw near with a
sincere heart in full assurance of faith, having
Our hearts sprinkled clean from an evil conscience and our
bodies washed with pure water. Let us hold fast
the confession
Of our hope without wavering, for He who promised is faithful, and let us consider how to stim-
ulate one another to love and good deeds, not
forsaking our own assembly together, as the habit
of some, but encouraging one another, and all the
more, as you see the day drawing near.*

It is true there are churches that are full of perfidy
(false to trust) because they are so wrapped up in their
narcissistic goals of "feeling good" gospel and enter-
taining that they fill their pews with people who know
nothing of obedient discipleship in Jesus Christ. Their
god is their belly. Flee from them. I pray that anyone
who takes time to read this little "magnum opus" will
be blessed beyond measure, not because I have prayed
over this material many hours and read many books, and
taught most of it in classes, but because of the message it
presents. I believe Jesus Christ is the only answer to our
need for forgiveness and cleansing by his transforming
power to save.

Psalm 139 tells us that whoever you are know that
God already knows your name, when and where you
were born and what you are doing right this minute. IT IS
TRUE, WE CAN'T POSSIBLY COMPREHED THIS,

BUT GOD loves you and is waiting expectantly for you to believe in him and his promises for eternal life, in the name of the Father and the Son and the Holy Spirit. God is seeking people who will worship him in spirit and truth. Take a stand dear friend. Read Romans 10:9-10 and say YES! to Jesus. Amen

Chapter 47

REJOICE WITH ME IN FAITH

How important is the message and information I leave with those who will read it and rejoice with me in faith and hope for a guaranteed future with Christ? On November 2nd, 2011, I received an email from one of our dearest friends, Angelo Rebizzo. Angelo received Christ at the Billy Graham Crusade in 1958. A week or so after his acceptance of the Father he started coming to our little church in San Francisco. It was clear to me that the Lord sent him to us. The church was just three years old. Think of it as David and Goliath in sin city. Angelo and his family started to attend our Sunday services. A few months later we started a home Bible study in the Rebizzo's beautiful, welcoming home.

I taught the Bible every Thursday evening for over a year at Angelo's home. I began in the Old Testament and related texts from both the Old Testament and the New Testament. Angelo invited his friends and family to come and we typically had from 12-18 who shared the evening. There were times when our discussions carried us to midnight. Angelo's wife Corrine served light refreshments. Everyone in the group made their decision to follow Christ. I baptized each of them and they became a vital part of our ministry for years. The church grew steadily as more people joined our ministry.

Angelo and his wife Corrine became life long friends to Dorothy and me. Our friendship has been steadfast over fifty years even though in later years we have seen each other infrequently. Out of the blue, in 2011, I received Angelo's email telling me he was dying of pancreatic cancer. I had never received an email from him before, so I knew it was urgent. Such news is always shocking to receive. What was important is Angelo's spiritual affirmation to God and readiness to await the Lord's call to take him home. In his email he said, "Gordon, I am at peace…and do not fear death. I am not looking forward to the "process" of dying… I don't pray for healing, but that the Lord will walk the path with me." Jesus said: " I will come and receive you to me, that where I am you may be also."

As I write this Angelo is with the Lord. I have tears of the loss of my dear friend, but joy that he is with the Lord Jesus Christ. On February 10th, 2012 I received an email from his daughter, Sharon. I married Sharon and her husband Glen Shanks years ago. Her email read "Home At Last." Angelo died on the 9th. Angelo told the family "Maybe today will be the good day" meaning the Lord would come for him.

I want to tell you, this is the way people live and experience life in Christ to the fullest. This is the way we are to face death. Jesus said: "…let not your heart be troubled, neither let it be afraid…I go to prepare a place for you and I will come again to receive you to myself that where I am you will be also." —John Ch. 14:18.

The Lord walked the path with Angelo. *"Dear long time trusted friend Angelo, have a great time seeing and visiting Dorothy and all our friends from the church I served, and I will join you soon."*

"Let not your heart be troubled neither let it be afraid."—John 14:1, 27 Amen.

Chapter 48

OBEY MY VOICE

I have been reading the *Commentaries of John Calvin*, by T.H.L. Parker. I came across a section where he talks about the significance of hearing God's VOICE. He says: "After we grasp the principle that God cannot be worshiped unless we listen to his voice, we must consider, as I said, what God's voice prescribes to us. Since he is Spirit, he demands the sincere love of the heart... he wishes us to call upon him for help, and to offer to him our praise...This is how we can distinguish true religion from superstition; when the word of God directs us, there is true religion." Jeremiah the prophet speaks to the people of Israel admonishing them to turn back to God; he commanded them saying: "Obey My Voice and I will be your God and you will be my people."— Jeremiah 7:21, 22

John Calvin's commentary on the Bible talks about God sending his only Son. Calvin calls this an 'irrevocable truth,' quoting: "Behold, my beloved Son, in whom I am well pleased; hear him."—Matthew 9:7. Further, Calvin says: "We know that from the beginning God desired spiritual worship, and that he has not changed his nature. Today he approves nothing but spiritual worship, for he is Spirit. But equally under the law, he wished to be worshiped with a sincere heart. God cannot be worshiped unless we listen to his voice...what God's voice prescribes to us." Later he says: "We know God, not to use him, but to worship and obey him. Therefore we know, not God's essence (as we know the essence of an object), but his grace and will by and for worship and obedience."

John Calvin has this to say about the Word of God: "Although we may maintain the sacred word of God against gainsayers, it does not follow that we shall forthwith implant the certainty which faith requires in the hearts, profane men think that religion rests only on opinion. That they may not believe foolishly, or believe on slight grounds, desire and insist to have it proved by reason that Moses and the prophecies were inspired. But I answer that the testimony of the spirit is superior to reason...These words will not obtain full credit in the hearts of men, until they are sealed by the inward testimony of the spirit."

Calvin again regarding the ETERNITY OF THE WORD: "There are those who will not dent the openly the eternity of God, but who secretly deny the eternity of the Word. It began long after God's existence. The Word only began to be when God opened His mouth at the creation of the world, that somehow the essence of God changed. This, of course is false because God always was, is and His Word was who God is. You cannot separate the Word from the Person. "Without the Spirit of God, you will never understand the things of God, for they are spiritually discerned." "They that worship God, must worship Him in Spirit and truth." (John 4:24)

I have been studying the Gospel of John in preparation to teach a class. In reading through a book on John by Arthur Pink several points regarding the use of the Word of God are discussed. Pink puts it like this:

A Word is a medium of manifestation,
thoughts turned into words is recognizable.
A Word is a means of communication,
by means of words to transmit information.
A Word is a method of revelation
by our words we are justified.

Words and thoughts go together. King Richard in Shakespeare's *Hamlet*, in the play within the play, Hamlet sets out to prove Richard killed his father in order to marry his mother. As the plot thickens Richard goes to his room to pray. He concludes: "My words fly up my thoughts remain below, words without thoughts never to heaven go." Lots of people have thoughts but are unable to connect the ideas with actions. People may have good intentions but they will never stir the heart of God. Hell is paved with people with good intentions. As a man thinks in his heart so is he. The heart with the mouth sends forth good or ill. That is why meditation on the Word and prayer go together. Does God hear us? Absolutely. How can we be sure? Because the Holy Spirit in us intercedes for us. Romans 8:16: "The Spirit testifies with our spirit that we are the children of God." More than that, in the same way, the Spirit also helps our weakness for we do not know how to pray as we should.

But, the Spirit himself intercedes for us with groaning too deep for words.

The Word was with God and the Word was God. The same was in the beginning with God. Jesus had his own personality separate from God. In him all the Godhead dwelt bodily. This destroys Gnosticism's idea that Christ was only in the mind of God; that he was not real. The Scripture makes it clear that the Word was eternally with God, and the incarnation proved his true identity with the Father; "I and My Father are One." Jesus was sent by the Father to do his will and in obedience to the Father he went to the cross. He momentarily subordinated his deity to die for humanity. "Who His own self bore our sins in his own body on the tree, that we, being dead to sin should live unto righteousness."—I Peter 2:24

Part IV

FAVORITE THOUGHTS AND VERSE TO SHARE

FAVORITE THOUGHTS AND VERSE TO SHARE

Einstein's definition of insanity: "To somehow expect something different when you do the same thing over and over again."

Dietrich Bonhoeffer wrote my favorite poem entitled "Who Am I?" His closing statement: "...whoever I am, thou knowest, O God I am thine."

WHO AM I?

Who am I? They often tell me I would step from my prison cell
Poised, cheerful and sturdy,
Like a nobleman from his country estate.
Who am I? They often tell me I would speak with my guards
Freely, pleasantly and firmly,
As if I had it to command.

Who am I? I have often been told that I suffer the days of misfortune
With serenity, smiles and pride,
As someone accustomed to victory.
Am I really what others say about me?
Or am I only what I know of myself?
Restless, yearning and sick, like a bird in a cage,
Struggling for the breath of life,
As though someone were choking my throat;
Hungering for colors, for flowers, for the songs of birds,
Thrusting for kind words and human closeness,
Shaking with anger a capricious tyranny and the pettiest slurs,
Bedeviled by anxiety, awaiting great events that might never occur,
Fearfully powerless and worried for friends far away,
weary and empty in Prayer, in thinking in doing,
Weak, and ready to leave it all.

Who am I? This man or the other?
Am I then this man today and tomorrow another?
Am I both all at once? An Imposter to others,
But to me little more than a whinnying, despicable weakling?

Does what is in me compare to a vanquished army,
That flees in disorder before a battle already won?

Who am I? They mock me these lonely questions of mine.
Whoever I am, you know me, O God. You know I am yours.

This is my favorite Psalm 103:
Bless the Lord, O my soul,
Bless His holy name.
And forget none of His benefits;
Who pardons all your iniquities,
Who heals all thy diseases,
Who redeems your life from the pit,
Who crowns you with loving kindness and compassion;
Who satisfies your years with good things, so that your
youth is renewed like the eagles.
Amen.

JESUS IS THE VOICE OF GOD. JESUS IS GOD.

When Jesus is confronted by the Pharisees and the teachers of the law. For them the law was the seat of authority so they asked Jesus: "By what authority are you doing these things, and who gave you this authority?" Jesus had just entered the temple and began teaching when the chief priests and elders, the most powerful leaders in the temple asked him this question. At this point they had obviously accepted the fact of his having performed miracles and witnessed his cleansing of the temple the day before. They did not need any more proof. There was authority in his VOICE and his Words. (Matthew 21: 23)

"BEHOLD, I stand at the door and knock, if anyone hears My VOICE and opens the door, I will come to him and will dine with him, and he with Me." — Revelation 3:20

The VOICES of the Martyrs

"And I heard a loud VOICE in heaven saying, "Now the salvation, and the power, and the kingdom of our God and the authority of His Christ have come, for the accuser of our brethren has been thrown down, who accuses them before our God day and night, and they overcame him because of the blood of the Lamb and because of the word (VOICE) of their testimony, and they did not love their life even to death." —Revelation 12:10-11

Their witness, their VOICE becomes our clarion call to follow in their steps:

Our certainty in salvation is in Jesus Christ, the Lamb of God, and the power of His resurrection, our hope and trust is in participating in His kingdom forever.

The Psalms constantly encourage one to SING praises to God and to take heed of HIS MIGHTY VOICE: *Let all the earth sing praises to His name and His angels continue to do His bidding day and night.*

The VOICES of the Saints

"Therefore, since we have so great a cloud of witnesses surrounding us, let us also lay aside every encumbrance, and the sin which so easily entangles us, and let us run with endurance the race that is set before us, fixing our eyes on Jesus, the author and perfecter of faith, who for the joy set before Him endured the cross, despising the shame, and has sat down at the right hand of the throne of God." —Hebrews 12:1-2:

Read carefully and meditate on Psalm 103-105. Psalm 103: 19: "The Lord has established His throne in heaven And His kingdom rules over all. Bless the Lord, you His angels, Who excel in strength, who do HIS WORD, heeding the VOICE of HIS WORD Bless you ministers of His, who do His pleasure, Bless the Lord, all His works, in all places of His dominion. Bless the Lord, O my soul." Amen.

FREEDOM: I was able to experience and enjoy the celebration of the Gorge W. Bush library on April 25,2013, in tears. The word that stands out most in my mind after watching the whole celebration on television is the word FREEDOM, what a blessed America we live in. What a joy to be able to say that I am an American. In our travels across America we will visit the Bush Library and the Ronald Reagan Library in California.

The river of blessings run deep in my soul. God has blessed our country with so many blessings they cannot be counted in an hour or a day. We are so blessed with our children and their children. As grandparents we are blessed beyond measure to have lived to see another generation born. *Jesus loves the little children...suffer the little children and forbid them not, for of such is the kingdom of heaven. Amen.*

The book of Hebrews keeps ringing in my head demanding my attention. Listen carefully to the opening verse of chapter one:

"God, after He Spoke (his VOICE) long ago to the fathers in the prophets in many portions and in many ways,

*In these last days has spoken (his VOICE) to US
in HIS SON,
Whom He appointed heir of all things, through
whom also
He made the world... when He had made purification for sins,
He sat down at the right hand of the Majesty on
high."* —Hebrews 1:1-3

Man can't say that he has never heard from God. His VOICE has gone out throughout the whole earth; "to the fathers in the prophets." Israel had its opportunity time and time again to get the Word out, but they failed to do it. But in the last days God intervened. God has spoken to us through his only begotten Son. He is heir of all things literally in heaven and on earth. He made purification for sins on the cross. His resurrection is the guarantee of ours when we believe. Study the book of Romans, Chapter 8. It tells of the real battle between THE LAW, THE FLESH AND THE SPIRIT. There is no condemnation to those who are in Christ Jesus. For the law of the spirit of life in Christ Jesus has set you free from the law of sin and death.

THE LAW: What does Paul mean by "THE LAW?" God established his laws right from the beginning. In Genesis he said," this you can do, that you cannot do lest you die." What happened? They chose to follow their own will (free choice) and thumbed their nose at God and ran away. The consequence was the judgment of God. They died spiritually and physically. From their progeny the whole human race suffered loss.

If you don't believe this ask yourself the following questions: when was the last time I ran a red light? When did I ever stop to help my neighbor in distress? When the speed limit is set in law at sixty-five mph. People ignore it and drive 75 or 80. When was the time you wanted something so badly, like a new car? Your wife said we need to wait but on your own you bought it knowing it would put you in a financial bind. Did any of these mirror your life? If you said *yes*, you are guilty and have to accept the consequences.

OMNIPOTENT, OMNISCIENCE: Without God's divine revelation man is a lost soul in the universe. BUT God sent his own Son who speaks to us with clarity. It is this Son, creator with God who came and offered his life as sacrifice for our sins that we might freely come to God and be saved. If you ever come to God it is not because you initiated it. It is because God seeks you out by his Holy Spirit. But if and when he comes to you and says: *Child, come to me, you are mine* don't hesitate a moment, take his hand and follow him. Be thankful he has picked you out amongst the crowd. "You have not chosen Me, but I have chosen you..."—John 15:16

This is God's voice speaking to us from the past to the present into the future. Here is the answer to life, health, purification and forgiveness for our sins to all who will receive God's Son, Jesus Christ, and all who will believe and trust him receives eternal life. It is all of God's doing. Romans 1:19:20:

"Because that which is known about God is evident in them; for God made it evident to them. For since the creation of the world His invisible attributes, His eternal power and divine nature have been clearly seen, being understood through what has been made, so that they are without excuse."

GREAT HYMNS

God's VOICE speaking, Wonderful words of Life
  "Words of life and beauty, teach me faith and duty."

I Can Hear my Savior Calling
  "Take My cross and follow Me."

I Hear the Savior Say
  " Child of weakness watch and pray. Find in Me thine all in all."

  I Heard the VOICE of Jesus Say
  Jesus Calls Us O'er the Tumult
  Jesus is Tenderly Calling You Home
  Speak Lord, In the Stillness
  We Have Heard the Joyful Sound

GOD IS THE LIGHT: Genesis 1:14-19: "God said, let there be lights (Greek-photo) to separate night and day." From this word we get all the different directives pertaining to light, photography; photosynthesis; giving life to plants to regenerate; giving new life. (Genesis 2:7)

THE LIGHT SHINES IN THE DARKNESS: When a person finds himself in the dark what steps does he take to get back into the light? If the power in his home goes out due to a thunderstorm, he immediately lights candles or turns on the generator. One can't get much work done in the dark, only the light makes work possible.

There is a double darkness man faces: the darkness when his natural light is gone, and the darkness he faces without God. Even when man has normal light for each day he is still in darkness spiritually. When Christ comes into our life the darkness we lived with is turned into new light and life. We are a new creation. The Holy Spirit of God comes to dwell in our hearts and turns our darkness into light. Where Christ is darkness must flee. He is the light of the world. Light is a metaphor for Christ. The Psalmist cried—"THE LORD IS MY LIGHT AND MY SALVATION; WHOM SHALL I FEAR HE IS THE DEFENSE OF MY LIFE."—Psalm 27:1.2

LIFE: "Then the Lord God formed man of the dust of the ground, and breathed into his nostrils the breath of life and man became a living soul."

- God formed man of dust
- Breathed into his nostrils the breath of life (spiritual)
- And man received a living soul (body, soul, spirit)

Before this happened there was nothing but a clod of dirt waiting for God's command. Man wasn't an amoeba in a slime pit that suddenly decided to be a human. Humans did not evolve through Darwin's process of evolution and natural selection until the time when we stood upright with arms, legs and feet. This is the Theory of Evolution of human beings which Darwin would have us believe. How preposterous is that? I wonder what Darwin said when he stood before God? Where did we get our brain and thought process? After you consider all the steps evolution had to endure for eons, God's explanation is much more logical and conclusive. A child was once heard to say, "God did it, my body."

SIN: Every person born into this world is a sinner. "Behold, I was shaped in iniquity, and in sin did my mother conceive me."—Psalm 51:5 This statement takes us all the way back to Adam and Eve, our first parents. From this point on "All have sinned and come short of the righteousness of God." –Romans 3:23 We missed the mark, as it were. There are none righteous, no not one. God being a righteous judge someone must pay the price to satisfy his righteousness. God does not accept sin or the sinner without payment in full. Man could not satisfy God in his own skin, he had to face the full judgment. But God, being righteous did not leave man without hope. Therefore, he provided the sacrifice necessary in sending his only begotten Son to become sin for us. *"Who His own self bore our sins in His body on the tree, that we being dead to sin should be saved by His grace."—1 Peter 2:24*

Man has to realize he is a sinner. How does this happen? Every person has a conscience. It registers right and wrong, good and evil. When a person jumps into a raging river to save a drowning man what triggers him to do this, or when one sees a house burning, what makes him run inside to save a screaming mother or child? Some people call this an automatic reflex to do the right thing. What makes us ready and willing to do the right thing?

Jesus identifies with sinners. He will be their sin bearer to the cross. His perfect righteousness will be imputed to us. II Corinthians 5:21 tells of the beginning of his public ministry and is full of meaning:

- The confirmation of the Father and the Son and the Holy Spirit
- His death and his resurrection are immanent (Luke 12:50)
- It prefigures the importance of baptism for Christians
- It marks his first public ministry and identifies with those whose sins he would die for. (Isaiah 53:11; I peter 3:18)
- It affirms his Messiah ship with the testimony direct from heaven with God's approval. (Matthew 3:16, 17) (JM)

The Old Testament story is about God teaching the Israelite the importance of offering to him animal sacrifices. God told them how, when and where it was to be done. His instructions were specific. And when the people became rebellious God rejected their sacrifices as unworthy. They were punished until they once again returned to God. It seems like this problem was generational. One generation worshiped God and then when the next one came along they rebelled and rejected him. *It's like, will we ever learn?*

SCRIPTURE: Scriptures were given to reveal the knowledge of God. It is his divine revelation about who he is, what he stands for and it is his direct conversation to us, his VOICE. II Timothy 3:16, 17: "ALL SCRIPTURE is INSPIRED by GOD and profitable for teaching, for reproof, for correction, for training in righteousness; so that the man of God may be adequate, equipped for every good work."

BELOVED: "My Beloved" is unique, one of a kind; there will never be another one like Him. Beloved can mean one loved by God or one who is loved.

FORTY DAYS, FORTY NIGHTS: IMMEDIATELY JESUS IS LED INTO THE WILDERNESS TO BE TEMPTED OF SATAN. How could Jesus go without food for this long period? What sustained Him? Moses and Elijah had a similar experience. They all were led by the Spirit of God who sustained them throughout their ordeal. What this reveals is that whenever we are led by God to do certain things he asks of us, whether it is for a short period or long, we can be certain his Spirit's presence will sustain us. What is fasting but the commitment on our part to allow God the time he needs to cleanse our souls and make us new creatures in Christ Jesus.

C.S. LEWIS: "There are only two kinds of people in the end; those who say to God "Thy will be done," and to those whom God says in the end "Thy will be done." All that are in hell choose it. Those who seek, find. Those who knock, it is opened." (his meditations)

"The more you obey your conscience, the more conscience will demand of you. The church exists for nothing else than to draw men to Christ, to make men little Christ's...God became man for no other purpose. It is even doubtful, you know, whether the whole universe was created for any other purpose."

Thy WORD have I hid away in my heart, that I might not sin against you. The Importance of memorizing God's WORD: When we read it. "Study to show thyself approved unto God, a workman that studies is not shamed, rightly dividing the word of truth."—II Timothy 2:15. "Thy WORD is a lamp for my feet..."—Psalm 119:11. "105 Thy WORDS gives light."—Psalm 130

Psalm 119:11: "I have hidden your word in my heart." The importance of studying God's WORD cannot be stressed enough. Most people do not consider taking the time to do this. They have busy lifestyles, managing daily chores, cooking, cleaning, running here and there to the grocery store, putting the children to bed, doing the dishes, taking out the garbage on its appointed day to be picked up, and on and on.

Isaiah 55:11, "So shall my word be that goes forth out of my mouth (God's VOICE); it shall not return to me void, but it shall accomplish that which I please, and it shall prosper in the thing whereto I sent it." This is a very important passage from Isaiah. First his Word will go forth throughout the whole world through his messengers, the prophets, the apostles, his chosen ones, evangelists, pastors and teachers. Nothing can stop it. Whether they are unbelievers, doubters, agnostics or atheists, nothing can stop God's word. It will prosper wherever it goes. The Holy Spirit will go forth, sent by Christ, and people from all over the world will accept his Gospel, and believe.

The WORD is God's VOICE speaking to us personally. Until we realize this truth many Christians, yes Christians, are not going to take it seriously. People in America go around saying they are Christian because, of course we are a Christian nation. Aren't all people Christians? No they aren't. Look up the word Christian in Webster's Dictionary, what does it say. "A Christian is one who is professing that Jesus is the Christ." He is a follower of Jesus Christ in obedience to His will. The true Christian has surrendered his will to the will of God in obedience. If you do not believe this you are not a Christian.

"Believe and you will be saved."
If you will confess with your mouth the Lord Jesus, and believe with your heart that God has raised Him from the dead you shall be saved. For with the heart man believes unto righteousness, and with the mouth is made unto salvation"

Here God has clearly revealed the way of salvation. One must exercise his/her faith believing what God has said in his Word. Confession means one acknowledges that he is God and Lord of creation. Scripture says, "No one can say that Jesus is Lord except by the Holy Spirit." When you ask an unbeliever if Jesus is Lord, their response is "I don't know." They can't bring themselves to admit this truth without God's help. Remember that the demons recognize Jesus. "Christians have this deep personal conviction, without reservation, that Jesus is their own sovereign and master. This phrase includes repenting from sin, trusting Jesus for salvation, and submitting to Him as Lord" (John Mac Arthur) No one is excluded from this truth.

"For the word of God is quick, and powerful, and sharper than any two-edged sword, piercing even to the dividing asunder of soul and spirit, and of the joints and marrow, and is a discerner of the thoughts and intents of the heart."—Hebrews 4:12 The contrast here is between those who believe and those who do not. For those who believe the Word of God is as refreshing as the water from a fresh water spring. It is soothing and nourishing to the soul. But for those who refuse to believe, it is like a two edged sword, they are facing judgment and the executioner's sword.

BAPTISM: John the Baptist is the forerunner of Jesus Christ. (John 1:19-28) He warns the people about the importance of being baptized. Many come forward to be baptized by him. He speaks of the one who will come after him, that is greater and more powerful than John, who is not even worthy to untie his sandals. It is Jesus the Christ, the Messiah. When he baptized the man standing next to him he says, "I baptize you with water, but he who comes after me, he will baptize you with the Holy Spirit. There were number of people watching what John was doing, including the priests, and questioned his authority. "Why are you doing this?" Are you that Elijah? John's reply, "No I am not." "Are you the prophet? And he answered, no. Then who are you? We need to tell our leaders who you are." John replies": "I am the VOICE of one crying in the wilderness, prepare the way of the Lord, make his path straight." The next day John saw Jesus coming toward him and said: "Look. There is the Lamb of God, who takes away the sin of the world." Isaiah 53 tells the prophet's prediction regarding the coming of the Messiah and what will take place when he arrives. John verifies this when he says BEHOLD, the Lamb of God who takes away the sin of the world.

FREE WILL: If God already knows what we are going to do before we do it and decides to step in and make a change where is free will? The great thinkers like Erasmus, and Calvin debated this back and forth. "It was traditional in medieval theology to write on "providence and free will." It was a stumbling block because it made man's freedom doubtful. So the theologians tried to reconcile God's providence with man's freedom and responsibility" (Calvin) Calvin comments on Acts 20:32: "Since Scripture teaches that we have sufficient help in God's power, let us be mindful that only they are strong in the Lord who renounce their sin, free will and lean upon him who alone, as Paul confesses rightly, is able to build up."

When in times of suffering and being in prison or in a dungeon, what was God's will or Paul's or any Christian who is persecuted? What did he intend by their suffering? The answer is, regardless of their circumstances it is important to know that God's providence was there. Calvin's point was to remind them that even though they lost their freedom, they knew in hope God's sovereignty prevailed. The Christian who has complete trust and faith in God's sovereign will for their life also depends upon his divine providence to help them through the storms of life.

Thank you God for being my Father,
Thank you Jesus for being my Savior,
Thank you Holy Spirit for being my
comforter and guide.

Remember it is all God's VOICE speaking through his WORD and by the Holy Spirit. Romans 15:5: "Now may the God who gives perseverance (endurance) and encouragement grant you to be of the same mind (unanimously),with one another according to Christ Jesus, so that with one accord you may with one VOICE glorify the God and Father of our Lord Jesus Christ."

Having been justified by faith, we have peace with God through our Lord Jesus Christ, through whom also we have obtained our introduction by faith into this grace in which we stand; we exalt in hope of the glory of God. BUT not only this, but we also exult in our tribulations, knowing that tribulation brings about perseverance, proven character, hope, and hope does not disappoint, because the love of God has been poured out within our hearts through the Holy Spirit who was given to us."

We are justified by faith,
We have peace with God, through Jesus Christ...

Mark 9:7: "Then a cloud formed, over shadowing, and a VOICE came out of the cloud, "this is my beloved Son, listen to Him." This alone should be sufficient evidence for every knee to bow and willingly confess that Jesus Christ is who he says he is; our redeemer and savior, and believe by faith, and accept his finished work for us on the cross.

A Family of Writers
My entire family—Dorothy, Dyer, Sharon, Curtis and Joy—are talented writers. They know how to express themselves with wit and soul. Dot journaled her

remarkable battle with cancer and close relationship with the Lord. Son Dyer has the blood of an advertising wordsmith running through his veins. His creativity has won him much wonderful recognition. Son Curtis has the gift of writing as well and I fully expect him to author a few bestsellers one day. I want to share the words of Dorothy, Sharon and Joy in the following prose pieces. Enjoy!

The Double Image
Dorothy Davis September 17, 1972

In my high school picture album is a photo of my brother and I standing in front of his 1943 Oldsmobile. But that is not all. Coming out of my side is a picture of the tail of our horse and the head is lunging out of my brother's side of the picture.

What is this…a double exposure? Our picture and the horse's photo is on the same film. On our old box camera there was no reminder to move ahead to the next frame.

Life seems to be like this. More and more as I grow older I see that inside are all the right ideas, but outwardly they never seem to match up. That is man's dilemma in a nutshell. I desire freedom but seem to have less and less time for it. I desire to be looked up to as a person of integrity and wisdom, but not many seek my advice. I desire money but never seem to make it big. I desire health and I find myself in a life and death struggle with disease. I desire to be fearless but am beset with all kinds of fears, mainly stemming from the fear of death.

This is life out of focus, a double image if you please. Now where does this man Christ Jesus fit into the scheme of things? This one thing I know, I need help from another world. All the men I have met fall a bit short of the mark. Oh, it's not their fault. I fall short and I disappoint them myself.

We seem to have two men living in this body, the seen and the unseen. The one on the inside has to pull it all together to keep the man on the outside composed. The two have to focus in on each other. But they need someone to do the focusing. Someone has to move that lever on the camera to focus in on the subject. The camera itself has all the machinery but is helpless to move it one inch.

I suggest to you that Jesus Christ is that man. The first man Adam failed us. He fell in the ditch when he was confronted with Satan. He was too much for Adam. He couldn't see through the plot. It looked good on the surface but he did not take time to be sure. Now, God comes back on the scene. "Let's bring man back into focus." But how? By sending a new man. Jesus gives up his life in heaven with the Father and says: "send me." He leaps into flesh and strides onto the planet Earth.

But now the test must come to Jesus. Adam had his test and Jesus shall have his. Satan went into counsel with all his army and war was declared on the Son of God. After spending thirty years on Earth he had not succumbed to evil. Satan appears on the scene in person. "I will trap Jesus into obeying me." The confrontation was in the wilderness where Jesus was hungry.

The timing looked perfect for Satan. Here is Jesus Christ in a weakened condition and vulnerable. Gordon's words: He has spent forty days and nights in the wilderness fasting and praying to the Father to make him ready for his earthly ministry. His humanity is now in a weakened condition both physically and mentally. Hit him now before he can summon the angels of heaven to his aid.

Satan attacked Jesus on three levels of a man's life. First, is the area of hunger for food, then in the area of pride and power, and finally in the area of worship. Jesus did not call upon his divine powers. This would have been a disaster for mankind. It was important for him to be tempted in all points just as man is tempted. He must win in every area in order to become our Savior and king. "Not by might or by power but by my spirit saith the Lord."

Satan said: "IF you are the Son of God command this stone to turn into bread." Jesus answered: "MAN must not live by bread alone, but by every word of God." Next the devil took him up to the highest place on the mountain and showed him all the kingdoms of the world in a split moment in time and said: "ALL THIS power I will give you and the glory of them: for that is delivered unto me: and to whomever I will I give it." "...if you will worship me all this will be yours." Jesus answered: "GET THEE BEHIND ME SATAN: for it is written, you shall worship the Lord (true God), and him ONLY shall you serve." Finally Satan brought Jesus to the temple in Jerusalem on a high point and said: "If you are the Son of God throw yourself down from here and God will send his angels to rescue you before you dash yourself against a rock." Gordon's paraphrase: See Luke's 4:1-3. And the devil left Jesus. Jesus is more than a conqueror over evil.

Satan left. Jesus stepped into his earthly ministry to seek and to save lost mankind. He healed the sick, the blind, the leper, and fed the multitudes. He cast out demons that wrecked people's lives. He raised the dead to newness of life. He talked at length about the kingdom of man. His visible kingdom was to arrive at a future date. This world was not ready for a visible kingdom. For three years there was a constant attempt to squeeze Jesus out of this world.

For now he made it clear that the kingdom was to be inside man, in his heart and mind and spirit. "You can set up a throne there and I will abide with you there. My spirit will be with you." "I go to prepare a place for you...that where I am you may be also. For now, I will send my Spirit and he will abide with you and teach you all the things I have said." That's what you call planning ahead.

So having made plans to come in the flesh he gave up his life with the Father for a reason. Why? He came to seek and to save the lost (mankind). Because Christ knew the forces of hell were set to try and rub him out, he let those crooks take him. But the grave could not hold him. He burst forth in his same physical form and was recognized by many witnesses. Every day as I walk through my garden I am remembering he is still breaking forth from that seed, that bulb, looking dead as it is, dropped into the cold ground, actually bursting forth and bringing with it food, beauty, everything it was intended to be.

I planted some squash seeds in the ground. Those seeds came forth with lush leaves, squash and even more squash came up. Finally we had to tear it out from the ground or it would keep growing. Nature doesn't seem to have any trouble fulfilling itself. Why can't man be like that? Why can't I be all the things I want to be, all that is pure and good and right? I don't mean the dark selfish things. Why? Because, I need someone who is greater than myself. I need someone who knows what my motives are and what they should be. I need someone I can trust myself to that has my best interests in mind. Where can this man be found? According to my Bible, Jesus Christ is the answer. He wrestled the giant threat to man and beat him.

Lord, I want to be on your side. I'm no match for this creep. He does me in. I need a greater person than I am in my life. So Lord, I'm telling you this and I am believing in you. I am over there on the winning side and I keep reading your word. Your word keeps giving me this insight. So Lord, please get a handle on the focus and pull it together. I'll just hold real still and you focus. I think the Bible calls that abiding.

Just hang in there and be a grape. At first you are just a seed in the dirt with all the vines and branches in that seed, all hidden from sight. Hang in there, you are above ground now. In fact, you are growing on my fence in our back yard. By golly, there is some fruit too. Just one bunch, but it is there and looks good. Now become what you are. God is on the throne. Hang in there. Let Him bring it all together. "Be still and know that I am God, Dorothy."

A Place To Sit
Joy Davis Houska, December 20, 1996

"Creek, creek, creek."

And again, dad's old rocking chair begins spinning the tale of its burdened existence. For nearly a lifetime it has, like Atlas, shouldered the weight of the world and whether providing support at the end of a hard day at work or offering idle comfort for so many football games, it seems as though the chair has always been there. Deep scratches on the armrest have been carved by the small occupied hands of certain children while watching Saturday morning cartoons. Over the years these canyons have become somewhat velvety to the touch. Initially carved by shaky unsure hands of the very same children, they are fading yet still visible.

Indeed there was a time when the wood wore a glowing varnish, but now the glow has receded to a mere dull sheen. The reckless use of the chair as a horse, car and countless other imaginary vessels have caused the reclining foot rest to tilt at an angle when fully extended. The reclining rocker is large enough to seat two small bodies, or one large one comfortably. It is and will continue to be the resting place for those bodies after many a weary day. Though in numerous ways the chair is looking more and more worn, a happy distinction lies in the fact that it doesn't mind the abuse. It now contains the living air that it did not possess when first it was purchased and that is bestowed only upon objects that have been much loved for so many years. This life quality comes with the wearing of the rough upholstery that clothes the chair. Initially the color of the chair was a vibrant red, but after enduring two children and a dog, re-upholstery is necessary. And though a multi-colored pattern dresses it now it does not make it feel in any way younger. Soon enough the old familiar smell of musty cologne settles back into the material, and the chair returns to the way it always was. Like a father it cradles the children and protects them from harm. There is a certain endless character about the chair that is reassuring. Despite the rusty joints, the ragged upholstery and the years of use the old chair endures and the creaking goes on.

The Joy of Running the Race
Sharon L. Davis

1 Corinthians 9:24b: "Run in such a way that you may win the prize." The day we are born we are automatically entered into the race and the day of our death we cross the finish line. There are two coaches who stand at the starting gate, one is a deceiver and one is a redeemer. The redeemer says the disciplined training will not be easy but the goal is worthy. The deceiver says we are all after the prize at the finish line. I will teach you short cuts and we will leave the others in our dust and will have fun while we are doing it. Those poor folks back there are still practicing the presence of God in their lives.

The redeemer asks his followers to do as he does. My Father, who is underwriting the race, has given me to you as your life coach. I ran the race with the other coach... he lost. Follow in my footsteps and the victory will be yours. This is not a sprint—this is a journey. Mind you, the other coach is going to play mind games with you and mess up your game plan. He tried that on me as well but I didn't fall for it. He is one angry coach and he is trying to beat me in the numbers game. He will tell you attractive untruths but I will tell you nothing but the truth. Truth does not always come in pretty packages.

You have several ways to respond to my instructions. It is your choice. The first way is OUT OF SERVICE; you do not believe; you are not plugged in or connected to my power and passion. The second way to respond to me is LIP SERVICE; you believe in me but the connection is shaky and the power often dims and goes out sporadically. The third way to respond is by LIFE SERVICE; you believe in me and my redemptive power. You are plugged in 24/7 to this power that runs through me to my heavenly Father who is the suitor and finisher of this race. As a result of his power your life becomes more and more of a selfless life dedicated to serving the physical, emotional and spiritual needs of others. I ran the race first for you. I stumbled to the finish line with a cross on my back. I had to cross the finish with the cross—oh so heavy—and yes, with your sins upon the cross. When you feel your burdens are mounting and the deceiver is accusing you and telling you that you are not good enough to win this race, you tell him that he has already been defeated by the same Jesus who lives in you.

My life coach doesn't just talk the talk he walked the walk and asked me to take the walk with him. Walking with him isn't always easy and the deceiver is waiting in the wings. It is practicing the presence of God until it becomes a lifestyle. It is following Christ in the discipline and discipleship until it becomes a lifestyle. It is listening to the Holy Spirit until it becomes a lifestyle and will prepare you to cross the finish line. With your eyes on Christ; the very one who you invited into your heart at the race track (some sooner than others). After all, we are a stiff neck people. Christ extends his nail-scarred hands with a gesture of welcome and well done to a good and faithful servant.

And One More Story…
The Gentle Cowboy

The lad puts on his cowboy shirt, slips into his trousers, tucks his shirt in and locks his belt tight around his waist. He picks up his holster and straps it to his side, grabs for his toy cap gun and a roll of caps for ammunition.

He slips into his shinny bright cowboy boots, stands up and looks in the mirror. He picks up his cowboy hat and adjusts it so it gives him a look of confidence and he is ready to meet any foe.

The cowboy is ready. He advances and drops down between the rocks. He hears a sound around the corner. He looks and suddenly he spots the enemy. He whirls around and jumps out from behind the tree and shouts, "I gotchya, bang, you're dead." He runs back for cover. Then he hears another movement on the other side of the giant tree. He leaps out and fires again, "BANG. BANG. BANG" and another phantom enemy drops to the ground, dead. The cowboy forgets he is standing out in the open. Another enemy jumps out from behind the tree and fires at him. The cowboy is hit in the shoulder and he drops to the ground. But as he is falling he fires his own gun and the enemy falls to the ground, dead. The cowboy brushes off his wound, stands up and walks away healed.

The fight is over and the cowboy runs back into the church where his daddy is waiting. He arrives home and goes to his room and puts his toy gun away and lies down on his bed and falls asleep to dream of other battles to be won.

His name is Dyer Gordon Davis.

God's VOICE: Thank you for Listening

When evening settles in and the reading of the daily paper is done. It is time for bed, and a sigh of relief. Who has time for the Bible? With a lifestyle like this people don't give God a thought. In my own life it takes concerted effort to put my thoughts of God in their proper place. Now that I am retired I read the Bible every day. I set aside an hour every day for prayer. I try not to let any distraction to keep me from doing this. It doesn't take a rocket scientist to figure out the direction our world is headed. I fear for our children and our grandchildren. What kind of world will they face ten, twenty years from today? I know I will not be here but for now I am going to pray for them every chance I get. Perhaps the Lord will come soon. I hope so. In the meantime we are to be steadfast, unmovable always abounding in the work of the Lord, because we know our labor is not in vain.

I trust this work will inspire you to study the Bible and memorize the WORD as the Holy Spirit leads. God's VOICE is more active today than ever before. Amen

Reverend Gordon K. Davis

ACKNOWLEDGEMENT

I would like to acknowledge all the people over my 85 years and counting who have enriched my life. Thank you from my heart to each of you who have guided and inspired my life's commitment to our Lord. A special shout out to my niece Vickie Dyer Abrahamson for her help in editing my words into *More Than Just Words*.

RESOURCES

And He dwelt Among Us: Teachings from the Gospel of John; Dr. A.W. Tozer

Bonhoeffer Study Guide: The Life and Writings of Dietrich Bonhoeffer; Eric Metaxis copyright

By Dietrich Bonhoeffer:

The Cost of Discipleship

Life Together: The Classic Exploration of Faith in Community

A Testament To Freedom: The Essential Writing of Dietrich Bonhoeffer

Commentaries of John Calvin; T.H.L Parker

Forgotten God: Reversing Our Tragic Neglect of the Holy Spirit; Francis Chan and Danae Yankoski

Gray Matter: A Neurosurgeon Discovers the Power of Prayer...One Patient at a Time; Dr. David Levy and Joel Kilpatrick

Holy Bible, New International Version, copyright 1973

Lange's Commentary on the Holy Scriptures; John Peter Lange

Love & Respect: The Love She Most Desires; The Respect He Desperately Needs; Emerson Eggerichs

MacArthur Study Bible; John F. MacArthur

Martin Luther's Basic Theological Writings; Timothy F. Lull

Mere Christianity; C.S. Lewis

Mounce's Complete Expository Dictionary of Old & New Testament Words; William D. Mounce

Scripture Alone and *Can I Trust the Bible?;* Dr. R.C. Sproul

Surprised By Joy: The Shape of My Early Life; C.S. Lewis

Surprised by the Power of the Spirit: Discovering how God Speaks and Heals Today; Dr. Jack Deere

The books of Biblical scholar F. F. Bruce

The English Standard Version Bible

The Presence and Work of the Holy Spirit; Dr. R.A. Torrey

The Quotable Lewis; Wayne Martindale and Jerry Root

Walter Brueggemann's bibliography of writings

CPSIA information can be obtained at www.ICGtesting.com
Printed in the USA
BVOW05s2102300714

360871BV00001B/1/P

9 781498 402552